Composites, Surfaces,
and Software

Greg Lynn &
Mark Foster Gage

editors

Composites, Surfaces, and Software:

High Performance Architecture

Yale School of Architecture
New Haven, Connecticut

Published by
Yale School of Architecture
P.O. Box 208242
New Haven, Connecticut 06511
www.architecture.yale.edu

Distributed by
W. W. Norton & Company, Inc.
500 Fifth Avenue
New York, New York 10110
http://books.wwnorton.com

Support for this publication was provided to the
Yale School of Architecture by Autodesk, Inc.

Yale School of Architecture
Publications Director
Nina Rappaport

Editors
Greg Lynn and Mark Foster Gage
with Stephen Nielson

Graphic Designer
Jeff Ramsey

The editors would like to thank
Dean Robert A.M. Stern

Library of Congress Cataloging-in-
Publication Data

Composites, surfaces, and software :
high performance architecture / Greg Lynn &
Mark Foster Gage, editors.
     p. cm.
ISBN 978-0-393-73333-4 (pbk.)
1. Architecture and technology.
2. Architecture—Technological innovations.
3. Composite materials. 4. Building materials.
5. Architectural design—Study and teaching—
Connecticut—New Haven. I. Lynn, Greg.
II. Gage, Mark. III. Title: High performance
architecture.
NA2543.T43C66 2010
721—dc22

                                    2010049421

Contents

Preface
Robert A.M. Stern
Dean Yale School of Architecture

Architecture since the Industrial Revolution has been influenced both by emergent technology from fields outside itself and by new materials migrating into the disciplines of building. But some of the most articulate proponents of modernism, such as Le Corbusier, enjoyed a relationship to technology that was as much symbolic as literal, looking to forms rather than processes, for inspiration. Others, less gifted as designers, like Walter Gropius and Konrad Wachsman, were far more literal, concentrating on techniques of assemblage. During WW II, and after, Charles and Ray Eames embraced new materials and processes of assemblage for artifacts, furniture, and houses. But they did not pursue this line of investigation for long, turning to other areas such as information management.

In the field of architectural education, the pursuit of technology as a source of inspiration can be seen reflected in the theories of the Bauhaus in the 1920s, if not in the practices which remained. In the 1950s and 1960s, at Yale, students worked with new materials—notably spray foam—but still the approach was hands-on and small-scale. Today, digitally-driven architecture promises a new scale of encounter—not an architecture of input and output that still holds too many in awe—but with the direct digital manipulation of actual materials to create new forms of enclosure and new kinds of decoration.

Greg Lynn, Davenport Visiting Professor at Yale since 2000, is at the forefront of this digital revolution. After a brief flirtation with "blobs," what could be called the "teenage" phase of digital design, Lynn came to realize that digital methods enhanced capacity to deal with the physical in a disciplined way. Lynn is attuned to the technologies outside the field.

Collaborating with Associate Professor Mark Foster Gage, ('00) Greg Lynn has taken the academic discourse to new levels of engagement with tectonics encouraging them to seek ways to cement a meaningful relationship between the digital and the physical, giving students the opportunity to meet with experts in the field so they might see, first-hand, how

digitally-driven tools are put to work in extra-architectural situations that demand high-performance design. In so doing, Lynn and Gage are enabling students to look at architectural problems in new ways, recognizing how sharing materials, tools, and techniques can strengthen the discipline.

This book is a compilation of that research and its implementation in a single semester-long studio. Focusing on the three topics of Composites, Surfaces, and Software, it includes essays by Lynn and Gage, and studies in automobile design (Chris Bangle, Adriana Monk); fabrication (William Kresyler); boat building (Bill Pearson); graphic and product design (Greg Foley); and of course in digitally-led architecture (Frank Gehry and Lise Anne Couture)—fields that have defined the performative cutting edge of today's technology.

As we consider the results of the studio, perhaps we can find a parallel between today's material exploration and that of earlier eras, but one that is less in the realm of symbols and more in that of direct experience. Will these explorations do more for architecture today than the engagement with advanced technology did for Modernist architecture in the early twentieth century? Or will it prove a diversion, taking architects away from age-old responsibilities to physical place-making?

I would like to thank those students—Lasha Brown ('08), Ashima Chitre('08), Jon Cielo ('08), Cody Davis ('09), Gabrielle Ho ('08), Patrick Lun ('09), Lorenzo Marasso ('08), Brent Martin ('08), Stephen Nielson ('08), Chiewhong Tan ('08), Quang Truong ('08), and Jessica Varner ('08)—who participated in the Yale studio and/or seminar and thereby contributed to this record of exploration. My thanks as well to Greg Lynn, Mark Foster Gage, and Stephen Nielson the co-editors of the book, as well as Nina Rappaport, publications director, for guiding the process. I would also like to thank our copy editors, Katherine Carl and Carolyn Deuschle, and graphic designer Jeff Ramsey, and W.W. Norton our distributor. In addition, all this would not have been possible without Autodesk whose generous support made the studio and this publication possible.

Introducing Composites,
Surfaces, and Software
Greg Lynn

Like many introductions, this one involves autobiography and anecdote.

During the last several years, at many of the leading schools of architecture, and at the Yale School of Architecture in particular, a high degree of facility in the use of the digital medium has been achieved. It has been my experience that often students translate the wireframe geometry from the medium of curve networks and non-uniform rational basis spline (NURB) surfaces architecturally into the structural framing, curtain wall mullion patterns and louvered panels of building elevations. Students have been taught to produce highly complex three-dimensional digital models whose curvilinear lineaments are converted to either the centerlines for structure or into panel patterns or grids from which elements are selectively deleted, altered, offset, or otherwise opened as apertures. Over the last several years, Mark Foster Gage and I have been teaching at Yale with an alternative approach to the architectural manifestation of these digital tools that rejects both the structural expressionism of turning wire frames into grid shells, and the layering of multiple surfaces with punched fenestration, brise soleil, and arabesque screens. Instead of complex structural framing or decorative aperture patterns we are consistently pointing the students towards preoccupations with massing, form, surface, and most importantly interior volumes.

Because we want our students to graduate a decade ahead of current practice so that they are well prepared for their present, we ask them to look towards alternatives to layered facades and complex structures that mimic the wireframe geometry of their digital files. So as not to continue to replicate what I consider a lazy translation of curve geometry into panels and tubes, we forbid the students to whimsically delete panels as punched windows, to design curtain walls with wireframe like grids, and especially we forbid them to rely on structural expressionism.

Since the late 1990s the louver has been one alternative to layering and wireframe structural grids as it divides surfaces along isoparms

(the lineaments defining the spline surfaces) and folds the surfaces at these points to make openings with directed views. Precedents for louvered surfaces are Herzog & de Meuron's Central Switching Tower in Basel, and my own hypothetical Embryological House as well as the North facade and interior of the New York Korean Presbyterian Church. The louver seemed a good solution to avoid structural expressionism and whimsical perforation, but after two decades it is now tired. The Yale studio discussed in this book looked beyond the tectonic paradigm of translating geometry into construction elements and proposed the topic of fusiform (tapered) hydrodynamic and aerodynamic precedents for surfaces.

This was a very unique approach for me as many years ago I imposed a prohibition on this very paradigm in an essay in *Animate Form* that attempts to define the difference between literal and phenomenal animation:

In naval design, for example, the abstract space of design is imbued with the properties of flow, turbulence, viscosity, and drag so that the form of a hull can be conceived in motion through water. Although the form of a boat hull is designed to anticipate motion, there is no expectation that its shape will change. An ethics of motion neither implies nor precludes literal motion. Form can be shaped by the collaboration between an envelope and the active context in which it is situated. While physical form can be defined in terms of static coordinates, the virtual force of the environment in which it is designed contributes to its shape. The particular form of a hull stores multiple vectors of motion and flow from the space in which it was designed. A sailboat hull, for example, is designed to perform under multiple points of sail. For sailing downwind, the hull is designed as a planing surface. For sailing into the wind, the hull is designed to heal, presenting a greater surface area to the water. A boat hull does not change its shape when it changes its direction, obviously, but variable points of sail are incorporated into its surface. In this way, topology allows for not just the incorporation of a single moment but rather a multiplicity of vectors, and therefore, a multiplicity of times, in a single continuous surface. Likewise, the forms of

North facade of the New York Korean Presbyterian Church

Greg Lynn

Janicki Industries factory floor for carbon fiber tool manufacturing

The Alan Andrews designed, carbon fiber, race boat Locomotion

a dynamically conceived architecture may be shaped in association with virtual motion and force, but again, this does not mandate that the architecture change its shape. Actual movement often involves a mechanical paradigm of multiple discrete positions, whereas virtual movement allows form to occupy a multiplicity of possible positions continuously with the same form.

Because I associated the design of boats and planes with primarily technical activity I thought it was important to prohibit the pseudo-scientific approach to the design of aerodynamic or hydrodynamic shapes as well as avoid literally dynamic buildings in favor of formally dynamic but inert solutions. Now, having learned more about how design software is used by naval architects it became clear that they employ these tools as a design medium not a black box of form-finding.

Mark Foster Gage and I knew from our teaching experience that if we instructed the students not to replicate the shapes of fusiform precedents that they might treat the digital medium as a black box to house the simulations and models they build. Then through a quasi-scientific method, which in actuality is an artistic process of happy accidents, students might "find" supposed optimized forms as if this was the same process by which boats are designed. To relieve them of this fantasy we visited one of the foremost naval architects of ultra light displacement boats (ULDBs) in the world, Alan Andrews. Alan and one of his designers Erik Berzins told us that in Alan's experience, "fast boats are always good looking boats," and that with experience a designer gains the intuition to see hull lines and forms that will perform well. The design intuitions of naval architects are verified and refined with physical tank testing at specific scales and through digital computational fluid dynamic (CFD) testing. Importantly however, hull, rig, and sail forms are not found; they evolve and are refined by design through the digital medium. We also found that in yacht design the use of software is in fact far behind architecture and industrial design in terms of sophistication of packages as well as facility with the software. What we discovered was that Alan and Eric wished they had more robust and precise software tools for surface modeling and that they had access to and expertise with computer numerically

controlled (CNC) model building equipment as well as three-dimensional rapid prototype printers for studying their designs in physical models and mock-ups. These are all design tools that our students are adept at integrating into their design process as well as into full-scale construction. The visit to the naval architects illuminated the role of design in the use of digital tools and dispelled the myth of the black box for optimized engineering. Although the elegant go-fast boats are designed using digital tools and CFD, their forms are not "found" in the computer.

More important than their influence on the students' thinking about design, the boat builders exemplified a new paradigm of construction and materials. The model for the structural frame and the layered facade is one of architecture's boilerplate assumptions, and through our examination of boat building we experienced an alternative paradigm of cooking discrete elements in a heated vacuum bag surrounded by a matrix of glue.

On our visit to Janicki Industries, one of the leaders in the manufacture of both composite shells and the tools to make them, we observed various stages in the fabrication of a number of very large, curvaceous, and bespoke components. Magnesium, titanium, stainless steel, Dyneema®, carbon fiber, and many other materials are placed in or on carbon fiber composite molds and plugs. These are pre-pregged, or covered in epoxy and polyester resin kept solid in refrigerators, and then baked in giant ovens and autoclaves at low temperatures, sometimes under pressure, inside a vacuum bag to infuse all of the parts in glue and to remove the extra weight of the glue where it is not required. Instead of attaching cladding to a structural frame or superimposing decorative layers, fibers are laid along load paths bonded with a variety of different materials all infused in a matrix of glue and cooked together into one composite. Often two or more layers of these composites are separated by lightweight core layers of foam, Nomex paper, aluminum honeycomb, or balsa wood to increase strength by adding depth between the structural skins.

When our studio convened in Nevada at the North Sails 3DL factory, Bill Pearson demonstrated how woven fibers placed along load

Image of the 33rd America's Cup winning BMW/Oracle Racing Trimaran

Detail of fiber path placement gantry at the North Sails 3DL factory in Minden, Nevada

12

Deck detail of BMW/Oracle Racing Trimaran

Image of flexible mold for flying shape of sail at the North Sails 3DL factory in Minden, Nevada

Detail of fibers of
a completed 3DL
North Sail

13

paths and baked into a rigid but infinitely formable surface in a bag under heat yields much more interesting outcomes than conventional processes. This is because the material result is not a painted solid surface but an extremely thin translucent surface riddled with complex lattices of curved fibers. Most interestingly, the molds are not solid plugs but massive flexible reconfigurable molds driven by a grid of threaded lifts forming immense curved surfaces. Arched fibers are placed across this using giant CNC gantry robots that lay custom fiber path sails that then convert to heating elements that bake this sometimes less than one millimeter sandwich into a composite. The results are the lightest, strongest manmade surfaces in history.

Inspired by the aesthetic of these composite materials that are combined into continuous surfaces as well as the beauty of the woven fiber path sails and their translucency, we defined a new composite paradigm that is in contrast to the much more familiar tectonic paradigm for architectural design. It is with this mission that we started the studio: the shift from a sensibility of tectonics to one of composites,

from layers of cladding on structural frames to laminated and glued lineaments of complex woven formations. To learn about the final product of these advanced processes, in Southern California we visited Westerly Marine, one of the premier custom racing sailboat builders, where we witnessed how composite elements come together and are assembled into a complete boat.

To gain first-hand experience with the product of these methods, the students sailed on Mission Bay in San Diego aboard "Abracadabra," a 90 foot long former America's Cup boat owned by Dennis Conner. The students were grinding in sails and sailing less than 25 degrees from, and faster than, the wind. This last experience was the most important in my opinion because at the core of the studio was the passion for the ocean, wind, materials, technology, design, innovation, and a connection to the history of making large objects lighter, faster, stronger, and more beautiful.

The midterm and final reviews reflected this circling around a broad cultural and technical field by including designers, manufacturers, and critics. Some like Chris Bangle, Paola Antonelli, and Greg Foley spoke to a broad cultural design perspective, while others like Frank Gehry, Kurt Forster, and Lise Anne Couture brought their disciplinary knowledge from architectural practice and history. All of the critics pointed out that the students brought passion for the cultural project of aesthetics and construction into their projects rather than trying to mimic boat shapes. It was very satisfying to hear our colleagues' responses to the students' work, which was not only their first introduction to the culture of composite fast yachts but also to a new paradigm for architectural design. The students were asked to suspend their tectonic habits of structural frames with layers of cladding and were asked to respond to a hypothesis of an architecture of lamination and glue. Rather than just a discussion of boat shapes and plastic materials the projects resulted in a "composite" paradigm.

The following chapters organized by the themes, "Composites" with essays by William Pearson, Bill Kreysler, and myself; "Surfaces" with essays by Greg Foley, Chris Bangle, and Adriana Monk; and "Software" with essays

by Mark Foster Gage, Frank Gehry, Lise Anne Couture—provide the context and rigor that has evolved a new paradigm.

Yale studio sailing in San Diego on Abracadabra, a former America's Cup boat owned by Dennis Conner.

Final Review at Yale School of Architecture, from left to right: Presenting: Quang Truong. Front row seated: Mark Foster Gage, Greg Lynn, Greg Foley, Ari Marcopoulos (obscured), Robert Aish, Frank Gehry, Stanley Tigerman, Meaghan Lloyd, Mario Carpo, Lise Anne Couture, Paola Antonelli (not pictured)

Greg Lynn

Composites

The science of composites is predicated on the idea that distinct materials, intelligently combined, will outperform any of the individual components. Certainly, this assessment relies on how you define "performance." Performance is not inextricably linked to the goals of lightest and strongest and is more accurately the effectiveness of meeting precise criteria with extreme accuracy. In some instances we are looking for any combination of strength, weight, cost, sustainability, smoothness, and so on. Because composites are designed to take advantage of the specific qualities of multiple materials, their accuracy can be nearly perfect.

In the following chapter we glean the expertise of an architect, a sailmaker, and a composite craftsman. In each case it becomes clear that communication is critical to achieving levels of performance previously unattainable. In a sense, a composite is only as strong as the intelligence with which it is assembled. Similarly, the complex network of information critical to the work of these authors relies upon intelligent communication.

Designers including Greg Lynn express forms heretofore unfeasible with even the most advanced available construction methods. They do so through an intricate and highly controlled web of communications between the designer, the machine, and the material. To that end, Lynn offers an essay on how robotics and the associated languages of machines are being learned by designers enabling not only control, but also specialized expertise in design. It is more akin to the cultural act of learning a new language than to learning a technical skill.

Today's racing yachts sail faster than ever before. In large part this is made possible through the ability to digitally analyze, test, and fabricate the sails. Through a convergence in digital simulation and robotically controlled production, North Sails composite sail manufacturer is able to build a sail to the exact prescription of a sail designer, fluidly adding strength along paths of stress and decreasing weight wherever possible. Bill Pearson, technical director, explains the material and performative efficiency of high-end sail manufacturing and the software and composites that

make it possible. Through a tour of his facilities Pearson proves the feasibility of the curved, the seamless, and the bespoke.

This section is concluded with a plea from the craftsman. Fabrication master William Kreysler illustrates how, through a spectacularly diverse range of expertise, the craftsman translates techniques across disciplines to exceed industry standards. He argues for the importance of the craftsman as translator between the dreams of the designer and the realities of construction, insisting that while robots and software clearly expand the realm of possibility in design they will never replace the craftsman.

Familiar composites like plywood, reinforced concrete, and medium density fiberboard (MDF) have worked exquisitely for years, meeting cost, strength, and material efficiency targets. Today, digitally driven designs look to a new smarter industry of high performance composites to tackle unprecedented challenges.

Composites

Greg Lynn

From Tectonics to Cooking in a Bag

The predominant example of entrepreneurial innovation associated with President Obama's Economic Recovery Plan was the "Cash for Caulkers" or Home Star Energy Retrofit Act finally passed by the House of Representatives in May 2010. If "plastics" was the word of the future in the 1967 film *The Graduate,* then today's graduates should understand the future of caulks and glue. Instead of hammering, bolting and screwing disparate elements together mechanically, this is an era of chemistry and cooking.

There is a sea change in the world of construction: the shift from assemblage to fusion. In material terms this translates into a move from mechanical to chemical attachments; more simply, things are built without bolts, screws, nails, and pegs and are instead glued. In formal terms this translates into a shift from discrete, freestanding, detachable elements into layers of materials, blended or filleted connections, and smooth curvilinear transitions between elements. Take automobiles for example—they used to be houses (coaches), with windows in frames, resting on a foundation (chassis). Now the body panels are folded and glued with reinforcing webs that are then glued and welded to hydro-formed, stamped, and extruded frame elements so that there is no distinction between panel and frame. The interiors are formed in fiber-reinforced plastics and composites. The exterior panels are metal and plastics of various strength, brittleness, and malleability. Similarly, aircraft used to be built like buildings with frames, cladding, and interior finishes and surfaces with wood and metal framing and panels. Now, contemporary commercial aircraft are made of three-dimensionally woven fibers and tapes on mandrels that are baked in autoclaves. Where load paths are higher, additional mattes and fabrics are located and layered. Reinforcing structural elements in addition to the surfaces are either baked in the mold with the skins or glued to the surfaces afterwards. All of these fibers, sheets, cores, tubes, and panels are held in place with resins and glues that are either pumped through the entire composite via infusion or injection, or in some cases "prepreg" materials are impregnated prior to assembly. These elements are then consolidated when baked under vacuum pressure. This is all not to mention Formula One automobiles or military aircraft that far exceed the plasticity of commercial products.

Interior of the forward fuselage of a Boeing 787 Dreamliner

20

These objects combine magnesium, titanium, balsa wood, paper, cardboard, Nomex®, metal and fiber honeycomb, aluminum foam, carbon, Dyneema®, Kevlar®, Twaron®, aramid and glass fibers, tapes and both 2D and 3D woven cloths consolidated in a matrix of resin and baked together under pressure in massive autoclaves. The combination and layering of these disparate materials into a continuous chemically or heat-baked object is generically referred to as "composites."

This shift in paradigm from a gridded structural frame clad in panels to layered and woven materials bonded one to another has formal and spatial consequences. Composites imply layers, weaves, and most importantly curvature. In architecture, because of plans and sections perhaps, the occurrence of force and motion is thought of on a horizontal plane (the plan) while enclosure and structure is thought of in the vertical plane (the section and elevation). The shift from the use of wooden models in the Renaissance to drawings has been extensively researched and reviewed elsewhere. From this we learn that with changes in media come changes in concept, changes in construction, and changes in form. This is all to say that the emergence of a medium (such as the digital tools used for sketching, designing, and documenting by those under the age of forty) neither leads nor follows the emergence of a formal and constructive paradigm (such as composite construction). In order to think about and create composites one has to use a medium that visualizes and describes woven lines and curvature.

Composites and computers are coincident and dependent. In my personal experience the digital medium was introduced into the design process through structural engineering consultants. While working for Peter Eisenman, a Yale colleague, from 1987, until 1992 on both the Carnegie Mellon Research Institute as well as the University of Cincinnati DAAP building, I drew plans, sections and elevations on semi-transparent Mylar over two-dimensional centerline drawings that had been plotted from our structural engineers' 3D computer assisted design (CAD) model. The reasoning behind this was that Peter wanted to create a torquing, twisting, curving interior volume and exterior massing through a series of uniquely three-dimensionally rotating blocks. The fact that digital media was introduced into architecture not as a medium but as an engineering rationale persisted for more than a decade. Because of this, the use of digital forms has often been justified through arcane explanation of data analysis or structural efficiency rather than through architectural ambition.

Architecture has always been at the forefront of thinking about how force and motion impacts inert material through forms of stability. At times these stable forms have taken the shape of structure, whether as vaults and domes, piloti and slabs, even nests of woven steel diagonals. All of these are both expressions of forces in form as well as geometry in action. However form, and even its structural consequences, is never just structure. It always includes an institutional message, a spatial consequence, and an aesthetic character—in other words, a vast constellation of architectural and cultural consequences. It is impossible to define an architecture of vertical forces from a planar ground without the geometry of extruded elevation projections from a plan. With a compass, one conceives of loads moving along arcing ribs and vaults, spreading

across compression rings and buttresses. With new geometric and descriptive tools of abstraction come new concepts of force and motion through form. The medium of curve networks and splines implies not only a new concept of cladding and structure but also new ideas about interior volume, massing, facade, ground, and movement through space in general.

Many have confused this collusion of geometry with lines of force and motion with structural engineering. David Billington, Professor of Engineering at Princeton University, teaches structures through the examples of engineering elegance in form and material and argues that it is elegance and efficiency that makes these structures beautiful. Many engineers and architects believe that well-engineered forms are inherently beautiful. However, there is no aesthetic discourse that would allow one to seamlessly link structure and beauty, as there is a wealth of hideous looking well-engineered form that exists as critique—for example the Firth of Forth Bridge. The elephantine form of the bridge overall, the discrepancy between sizes of structural members, and most of all the collage of masonry and steel structure at the pylons is profoundly inelegant and in contradiction to Billington's aesthetic/structural discourse. One could go on with marvels of engineering and architecture from the NASA hangar at Moffet Field, to Louis Kahn and Robert Le Ricolais's project for City Tower, to Fazlur Khan and Skidmore, Owings, & Merrill's Sears Tower, all of which are ungainly, disproportionate, collided, juxtaposed and/or bundled structures that, while impressive feats of engineering and even design, remain aesthetically anything but elegant.

What made Robert Maillart's bridges at the turn of the twentieth century beautiful was not their structural expressionism but in fact was more akin to what Heinrich Wölfflin, in his 1888 book *Renaissance and Baroque,* argued as dominant in the Baroque—the dynamism and energy contained in their discrete monolithic form. The curves and surface of Maillart's bridges are taught, tensioned like bows, sprung with energy and movement. The spanning strength this provides, the dynamic movement of the eye across them, and the reduction of material in favor of lightness and optimization are not even their most important

Greg Lynn

Scotland's Firth of Forth Bridge, which opened in 1890, was designed and overseen by Sir John Fowler, Sir Benjamin Baker, and Allan Stewart

Salginatobel Bridge designed by Robert Maillart in 1930

aspects. Their significance lies in the details of dynamic forms, efficient tectonics, and elegant sculpting of surfaces (read somewhere between linear and curvaceous erring neither on the side of the emaciated straight nor the bulbously zaftig). These were not conceived in plan and section with vertical gravitational force but were conceived more three-dimensionally and with a complex nexus of views. Maillart's bridges have a character of litheness associated with engineering, but their curving and twisting surfaces have a sculptural character that can be seen from a variety of orientations. What makes them beautiful for Billington and for anyone with an eye to Baroque continuity and change in form and space is not their engineering but their design. The allure of these structures are generated from the careful consideration of the form's orientation as it relates to motion, its connection to the ground, and the continuity of elements as well as discrete edges, planes, and elegant surfaces. They are bridges, not buildings, but in aesthetic and real material terms they are composites and in formal terms they anticipate the kinds of curvilinear forms made possible by digital design technology.

By adopting digital technology, engineering now operates in the paradigm of composites. Instead of focusing on materials and optimal forms, it is perhaps better to look at the design medium. This medium entails curved surfaces, lamination of disparate elements into variable thicknesses and opacities, and most importantly shaping interior volumes through flexible surfaces that are folded, molded, and curved. This shift from the dynamics of the plan and the statics of the section to a pliable multi-dimensional space of curved surfaces is one of the most significant shifts in the way we think about architectural space since the invention of perspective.

Now the question must be asked: why boats? They share many of the characteristics of the Maillart bridges in their litheness and multi-facetedness. Also, admittedly I like to race sailboats more because of a passion for the forms, shapes, and materials than for the competitiveness of sailing; the principles and thinking behind their design compels me. One more personal anecdote about the transfer from boats to architecture involves the curves of a ship. While an undergraduate student at Miami

University of Ohio, I met a German exchange student who had some unusual drafting tools, one of which I had never seen. He attended the school because of its well-known Beaux-Arts watercolor section-drawing studio. For this he had a specific set of tools for drawing the non-radial curved vaults of his domes and ceilings. Instead of using "French" or "Ships" curves for drawing curved lines, he had a rubber strip with metal disks with crosshairs bonded to it at regular intervals. He called it a "Rubber Spline" and the metal crosshairs were aligned to crosshairs on a drawing so that the rubber curve took up a resulting shape. Larger "Rubber Splines" at scale were used to increase the scale of the curves in drawings. I later found that this Spline tool came from the ship building and the naval architecture industry and was also used by civil engineers. I collected a series of these tools that I had to special order and procure from across the United States, Europe, and Asia. Finally, at Princeton University a few of us used these tools for our designs. Then while using CAD software I discovered the MicroStation® package by Bentley® that had Spline modeling tools for use by civil engineers with the same set of handles and curves that flowed through them, but were digital. The connection between boats and buildings stems from these experiences with shipbuilding and drawing tools and with sailing antique wood boats as a young boy. Today in addition to the desire to explore a new composite logic of form and space I also feel the impetus to be part of the recent cultural history of architecture and design. The racing sailboat industry is one of the most innovative fields relative to architecture in scale and cost of construction today. In the same way that WWII innovations trickled down to the building, furniture, and industrial design fields fifty years ago, today America's Cup innovations make an impact on these same fields. This is in part due to the fact that a production sail boat costs less per square foot when measured in their footprint than an average building.

Then finally one could say that the focus on sailboats is contextual as our site at the Gasworks Park in Seattle is on the waterfront at the boundary between architecture, landscape, the sea, and the industrial ruins of the gasworks that demands a contemporary technological response. Having visited the factories with their massive computer numerically controlled

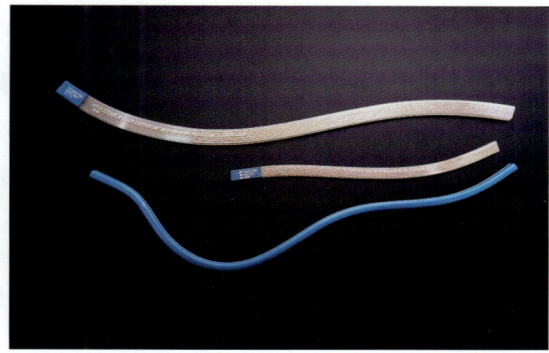

"French" or "Ship's" curve

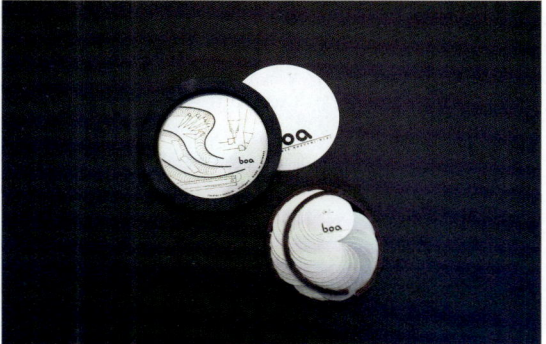

23   "Rubber Spline"

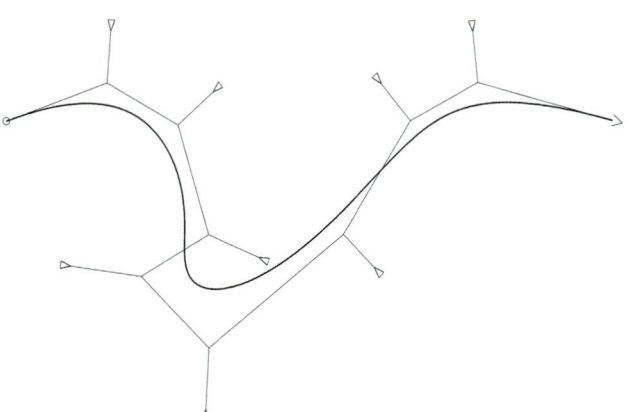

Drawing of a spline based on Bentley MicroStation spline modeling tools

(CNC) robotic arms and gantries we suggested that the students could express and expose these contemporary machines on the skyline and to visitors to the yard and showroom and also to celebrate these machines in the design of their enclosures. Furthermore, this location allowed for a silhouette on the skyline that was not a vertical tower but a profile more akin to a bridge or landform at the edge of the city. By tasking the students with designing a factory and showroom in the city they were charged also with bringing contemporary materials, construction, forms, and industry back into the city and into dialogue with the waterfront as well as the surrounding urban fabric.

The studio combined the use of surface modeling tools as a design medium with a design paradigm of composites. Because of the combination of relatively low cost with the need for lightness and strength, the racing sailboat industry is perhaps the best place for architects to look at composite construction at building scale and at the scope and cost of building construction. It was also valuable to meet naval architects as they are very much like us. Unlike aerospace, which is entirely digital and engineer driven, or automobile design, which is driven by styling while remaining recalcitrant to energy and material innovation, the boat designers combined intuition, common sense, innovation in typology before shape and struggle to integrate digital media with drawings in much the same way as the students. For centuries boats and buildings were conceived in the same tectonic fashion, as a frame clad in an envelope. Architecture can now learn from the naval architects who are fully immersed in the language of composites. It is the shift from multiple discrete layers hung on a frame to disparate materials layered and filleted together and cooked into a single composite that is most provocative for all of us.

Greg Lynn

Composites

William Pearson

North Sails Three-Dimensional Laminates: The Shrinking Space Between Composites and Textiles

As the boundary between textiles and composites has blurred, the term "flexible composite," once an oxymoron, has become the norm, at least in the sail-making industry. Fabrics with built-in three-dimensional shapes first developed for the sails of racing yachts, have been put to use in many other fields.

This performance sail material is flexible, extremely light, and can carry very high loads across its surface. Heretofore little known outside the world of performance sport, it has caught the eye of aerospace engineers and architects. Now, it is being introduced in cross-disciplinary collaborations with leading theorists and practitioners in their respective fields. The future potential of textiles and fibrous systems in architecture and building construction is significant because they provide differentiation through aesthetics and performance.

Sailmaking has historically been linked to textiles. Early sails were woven from palm fronds before the shift to flax fiber and cotton. Madern manufactured performance textiles such as nylon, polyester, para-aramids, and liquid crystal polymers are produced as fabric roll goods which are designed to be strong in one or two directions specific to the grain of the material. Because of varying non-linear stress paths on a sail, these swarths of fabric can only be arranged to approximately address the very specific demands for strength and lightness in a high performance sail. The symmetry of the zero-to-ninety grid (warp and weft) has been replaced by varying spatial fiber density and seemingly random orientations. Employing continuous uninterrupted fiber paths, today's one-piece molded sails are seamless, unitary structures.

3DL™ (Three-Dimensional Laminate) sails are made in a single piece on an enormous adjustable mold, to the precise aerofoil shape that is ideal for each yacht and application. Bespoke fiber placement is executed with the 3DL manufacturing process on a large scale on some highly unconventional equipment at North Sails Nevada. Sailboats range in size from approximately 3.5 meters to 66 meters in length at the largest. The sail size can be as large as 1000 square meters. The largest mold, and therefore the largest single piece membrane, is about 500 square meters.

Fiber-laying gantries travel over the surface of the sail molds laying down carbon and aramid fibers on a polyester (PET) film. This new technology revolutionized a process that had been the same for many thousands of years. Previously, individual pieces of symmetrical woven material could only be joined together by stitching or gluing.

Stronger Structures

These new high tech laminates contain several layers of film, resin, and reinforcing fibers such as carbon, aramid, and Ultra High Molecular Weight Polyethylene (UHMWPE). These high strength reinforcing fibers give the sail enormous tensile strength, and the PET film provides a continuous substrate for bonding and resists shear loading.

By carefully choosing the constitution of each layer, sail makers can prescribe the mechanical properties of the resulting composite. The resistance of the fabric to stretching (modulus) is especially crucial, as is the breaking strength, and yield strength (the load beyond which the material is permanently deformed).

Fibers that run continuously from one corner to another provide the structure's backbone and are laid in a pattern that exactly anticipates the forces of the wind. As a result, the sails maintain their optimal three-dimensional shape during use, and this structure also allows the sails to carry astronomical loads. Loads vary with sail size, type of boat, and strength of the wind. The corner loads on many racing sails are in excess of 10,000 pounds. The load on one corner of a big sail measuring 500 square meters on a large boat approximately 50 meters long could be 20,000 pounds. The specificity of the design and manufacturing technique represents the most radical advances in the fields of textiles and composites today.

Unlike the formal symmetrical structure of woven fabrics, this process embraces asymmetry, making the lightest possible sail by putting fiber only where it is needed. The placement of the fibers reflects the anticipated wind forces and variations of the stress field and also optimizes localized strength and stiffness. Although sail designers and engineers generally decide where the fibers should be placed, for the sails that are used at the highest level of competition,

William Pearson

Composites

it is the sailors who provide crucial feedback about what does or does not work.

In traditional textile manufacture, the symmetry of the zero-to-ninety grid requires that fiber be positioned evenly throughout any structure, not because of the requirements of the structure or product, but because of the requirements of the textile manufacturing process. By placing fiber only where it is required, this new world allows for better material economy. Better material economy allows for: lower weight for the finished product, which is important for performance applications; lower price because less material is used; consumption of fewer resources. Because material is placed only exactly where it is needed, this allows North Sails to use the world's best, highly specialized, expensive materials efficiently, on an as-needed basis. In this new industrial revolution we move beyond the idea of mass production, and its associated mass waste, toward individualized production or "mass" customization. There is no longer any distinction between the sail and the sailcloth; now both are made simultaneously.

29

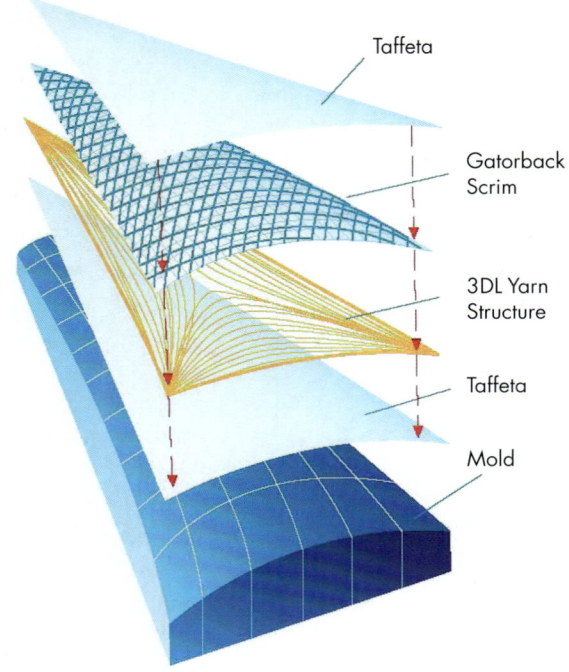

Taffeta

Gatorback Scrim

3DL Yarn Structure

Taffeta

Mold

In this diagram of laminated sail the discrete components of the composite can be seen independently. Gatorback Scrim and 3DL Yarn are placed between two layers of Taffeta.

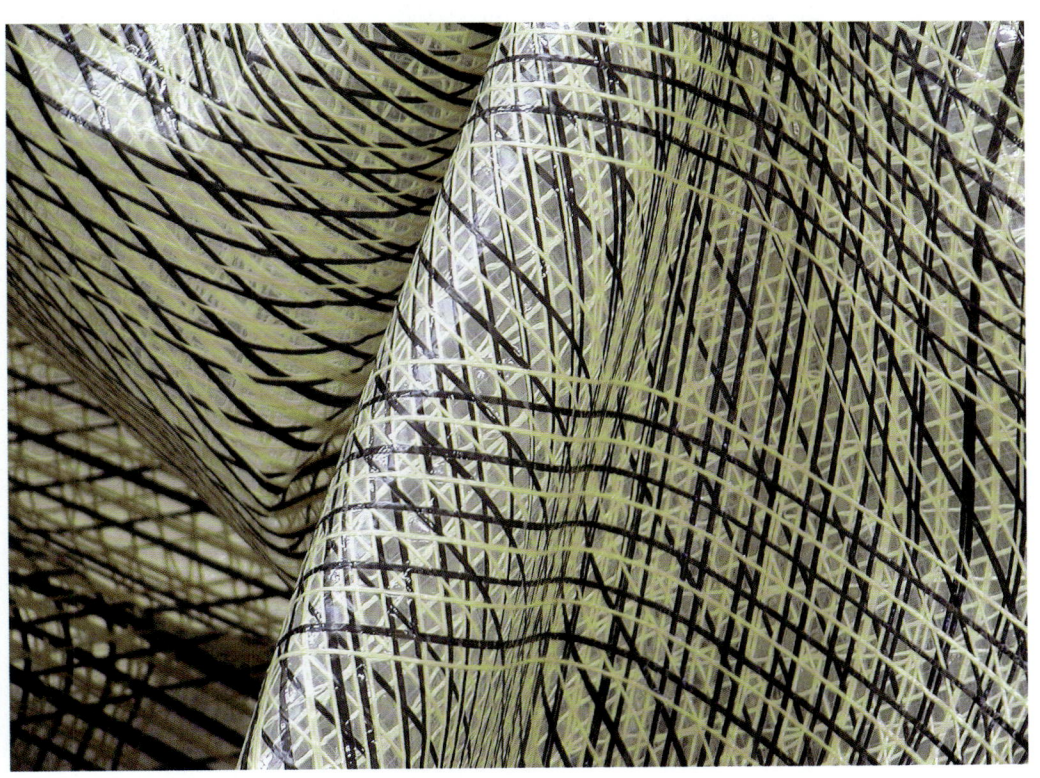

The bespoke fiber placement process allows hybrid blends of different fibers to be used in varying trajectories, densities, and orientations as required. This image shows a hybrid laminate made of carbon and aramid.

Varying spatial densities can be seen in this carbon fiber laminate.

William Pearson

Composites

In view are three of 3DL's eleven large horizontal adjustable male molds. The largest mold is 40 meters long by 19.5 meters wide. A 3DL sail begins with a three-dimensional computer aided design/computer aided engineering (CAD/CAE) file created by a North Sails sail designer. North's proprietary design software creates a custom "mold file" for each individual sail. A design file is then converted into programmable logic controller (PLC) machine code, which instructs the machine to render the mold in the designed three-dimensional shape.

At the heart of the invention is the articulating mold that can be adjusted in three dimensions to match the complex curvature of a custom sail configuration. The surface contour of the mold is achieved with dual pneumatic actuators controlling 350 lifting mechanisms, which drive an attached vertical worm gear one-quarter of a turn at a time, adjusting its lifter one millimeter per turn. This fine-tunes a segmented surface structure made up of parallel rods or battens and supporting crossbars covered by closed-cell neoprene foam that provides an insulating base layer for layup. The foam tool bed is covered with a loosely

fitted, metallic nylon sheet that reflects through the part during infrared heating and curing. The lifters operate like extension mechanisms that raise work platforms aloft for tree or utility line maintenance. As the lifters raise and lower, the segmented surface adjusts its position accordingly. Dedicated software enables the lifters to continuously poll each other and make very fast simultaneous corrections, so the entire adjustment takes place in only eight minutes.

Technicians oversee and participate in the manufacturing process from a horizontal position above the mold. As they lie in a hang gliding harness suspended from an overhead gantry, they follow the progress of the fiber placement head as it travels over the surface of the mold in computer-controlled pre-determined patterns.

After a base layer of PET film with a thin layer of thermoplastic co-polyester resin on the top is draped over the mold and tautly secured, a six-axis fiber head suspended from a computer-controlled overhead gantry applies structural yarn made of carbon, aramid, and UHMWP onto the surface of the base film. Its pattern follows the specified primary structural loads

Overview of the 87,000 square-foot plant in Minden, Nevada

The underside of a 3DL articulating mold

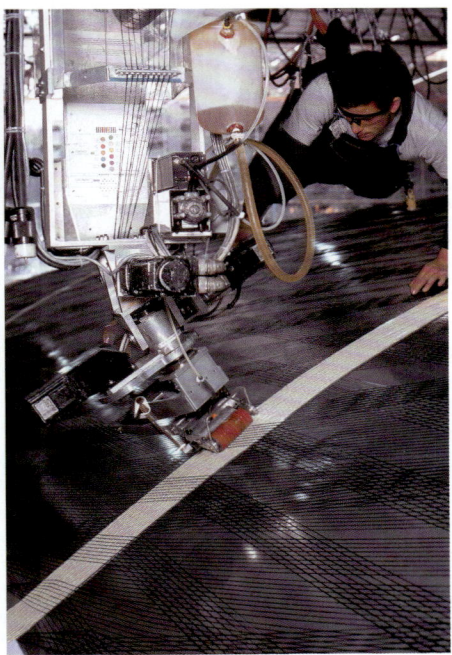

An operator follows the progress of the fiber placement head

Large sail on a mold after completion of the fiber placement process

Building the vacuum bag around a prepared membrane

Laminating an aramid racing sail

William Pearson

Composites

and the three-dimensional curve of the mold surface. The fiber head "draws" a pattern in yarn that matches anticipated loads in the sail. All structural yarns are applied under uniform tension and adhere to the surface of the film to ensure they remain in place since they will become locked in their location by the lamination process. The fiber passes through a twenty-millimeter wide resin chamber and segmented roll-coating device on the head. The resin is formulated so that it does not penetrate or permeate the yarn; it only coats the surface. This allows slight filament movement within the cured laminate, thus creating a "flexible" composite structure. The fiber placement head is attached to the bottom end of a vertical travel device called a Z-Car, which is suspended from an overhead gantry that runs the length of the building. Attached to the Z-Car is a climate controlled Plexiglas enclosure containing thirteen, three to ten pound spools of yarn.

During yarn placement—an operation that can take from two to forty hours, depending on the size of the sail—workers begin building the vacuum bag by first laying breather felt around the perimeter of the mold and then attaching vacuum ports through the felt. Once the yarns are laid, a second film is positioned on top of the base film and structural yarn. This is tensioned and then covered with a large vacuum bag film that compresses the laminate at approximately 14.7 pounds per square inch. The second film contains a secondary mapping of yarns to handle incidental loads not incorporated in the primary load lines and to improve resistance to tearing.

After the structural fiber is in place, and the secondary film applied, a vacuum bag is built around the laid up sail, before lamination begins. In process similar to that used in the manufacture of rigid composite parts, the lamination system involves creating a vacuum between two layers of thin film that encase the fiber structure and resin system. This forces the components together to consolidate the laminate, drawing out any air that would create voids in the finished product.

The part is now ready for lamination. The fiber placement head is then removed from the gantry armature and replaced with a carbon element heat "blanket" that cures the pressurized laminate by conducting a care-

fully controlled amount of heat through the laminate. This causes the laminate to conform tightly to the mold (thermo forming) in a manner similar to the shrink-wrapping process and also wraps PET film around individual fiber bundles, locking them into position in three-dimensional space. After curing, the sail is allowed to post cure further for a full five days prior to shipping and/or finishing.

In addition to the machinery that has been developed in recent years, it is the premise of asymmetry that allows this process to yield such efficient and high quality results. Again, the specific placement of the fibers in the sail membrane can be calibrated precisely instead of being applied uniformly across the surface. The use of continuous fiber and a three-dimensionally molded shape creates a sail that is lighter, stronger, and more stretch-resistant than anything that has come before. This allows the sail to better retain its aerodynamic shape over a wide wind range, and for a longer period of time than was previously possible. This results in a new era for producing sails that can be customized as a matter of course and are highly efficient in their material consumption.

3DL sails in use on a racing yacht during the annual Key West Regatta sailing competition

Bill Kreysler

Craft in
Digital Design

A chisel in the hands of an unskilled worker is a weapon. 3D modeling software can be equally dangerous. Like Renaissance painters who invested years mixing colors before they picked up a brush, today's designers would benefit greatly by understanding materials and their methods of fabrication before manipulating these powerful twenty-first century chisels.

In today's renaissance of design and fabrication, 3D modeling provides designers control over building systems so that complex shapes can be managed better than traditional forms using traditional design tools. For example, today's architects coordinate the electrical, plumbing, and heating, ventilating, and air conditioning (HVAC) systems in a compound curved wall in ways not dreamed of only a few years ago. With finite element analysis (FEA), engineers calculate and predict their structural behavior as well. Times are indeed changing, and we are pioneers at the dawn of a new method of building that frees us from the rectangular world of two-by-four studs, four-by-eight sheets, and the ubiquitous, but in many ways inefficient I-beam. Yet there is a dark side to all this opportunity. As extraordinary as these new tools are, they come with an entirely new challenge. Eliminating the need for two-by-fours requires replacing them with something. Creating a wall with curves requires that I-beams be invented that follow these lines, or perhaps it requires an entirely new and bolder system of monocoque structures with no internal frame at all. This freedom of design, as liberating as it may seem, is a handicap that will inevitably bring the walls crashing down, perhaps literally, on designers who do not employ in their design an informed and effective understanding of means and method. Today's tools do not make these complex buildings easier to design. They simply make them possible. The pressure and demands on the designers of today who wield these tools is greater than ever before. In the past, architects could rely on contractors to "figure out means and methods." Today, architects are far ahead of most contractors and are therefore exposed to the traps, dead ends, charlatans, and predators encountered by explorers of any age.

As a fabricator of composite materials for over thirty years, I am excited to see so many schools and design firms investing in computer numerical controlled (CNC) mills, rapid

prototyping machines, laser cutters, 3D digitizers, and other "tools of the digital trades." It is heartening to see that the need to develop craftsmanship has not gone unnoticed. Just as eighteenth- and nineteenth-century carpenters were hired based on the way their tools were sharpened and how they held a mallet, architects of tomorrow will be judged as much by their facility with the manufacturing techniques and materials they specify as by their designs. Indeed, designs of the greatest breadth and creativity will only be realized by those who understand how to build as well as what to build. The most successful will be those who have the combination of creativity to imagine great forms, the craftsmanship needed to get the most out of materials, and the new tools to assemble and create them.

However, is this possible? The craft of shipbuilding took centuries to evolve the best joints, splices, cleats, and fasteners used by boat builders today. The first idea is rarely the best idea. The job of crafting something is complex. In this rapidly evolving design and manufacturing environment how can craftsmanship be acquired quickly enough? From where will it come? There are dozens of ways to hold two boards together but there is only one "best" way for a given situation. One must take into account the materials, their mechanical and physical values and limitations, and know why the boards are being held together in the first place. Are they in shear, bending, or in tension? How will they move? Can they be allowed to move? If so, how much can they move? What are the environmental exposures? Is it even possible to put them together as designed? What are the tolerances of the surrounding work?

How will designers of today tap into the skills of the craftsman? How will they use their newfound software tools to create more natural forms, not just for their beauty but also for their efficiency?

Fortunately, hidden in the crevices of industrial parks, urban centers and their outskirts, are tradesmen who have learned their trade and who have added passion, dedication, years of experience, and often genius to take their work to a new level. They have the same passion for discovery and for exploring the unknown as our new breed of architects. They often use

Bill Kreysler

Composites

similar software. They have the technical skills to make things and are hungry for projects that challenge them. These are the craftsmen of the twenty-first century with whom designers should connect. Skill handed down through the ages is the key to providing design professionals with the means and methods to bridge the gap between their vision and the building methods of the last century. The shackles of the industrial revolution with its automated manufacturing and "economies of scale" are being challenged. The curved walls of new buildings cannot be made with plywood or sheet rock, nor can they be supported with straight beams or boards. Contemporary architects find they must rely on Renaissance skills to hand trowel on plaster rather than to nail or screw up flat sheets. Some architects are even resorting to things like custom-made I-beams, plasma cut out of sheets and welded together. In the process, they totally demolish the economy of the original manufacturing process in their attempt to blend contemporary forms with traditional methods. Certainly, there are better alternatives.

Often change comes with a new tool. It could be said that the invention of the composite bow by the Asiatic Hyksos people enabled the conquest of Egypt's twelfth dynasty; Henry V's longbow crushed the age of chivalry in one afternoon at Agincourt. In the field of construction, 3D modeling programs and their cousins the CNC tools are nothing less than such a weapon. With digital fabrication, custom-made products can optimize material usage and reduce environmental impacts, thus becoming cost competitive. In Bay House (see photos), reinforced plastic "sandwich" panels were a more economical and environmentally efficient construction method than traditional materials. Nineteenth- and twentieth-century methods of building from a catalog of prefabricated parts is challenged today by the notion that talented designers using powerful new tools working with contemporary craftsmen who can manipulate these new tools, will breathe new life, vigor, and efficiency into the built environment. This is not a new concept. From the pyramids of Egypt through the Dark Ages and the Renaissance, up to the Industrial Revolution, designers and craftsmen have worked hand in hand, often blurring the distinction between the two. Automation and techniques of mass production have been only a temporary

disruption to this natural and logical collaboration between designer and builder. Certainly, robots and digital tools are very much a part of mass production techniques, but these same tools can turn the supply and demand cycle upside down. Conventional design looks to catalogs and magazine advertisements for inspiration. Someone invents a new fastener, puts an advertisement in a magazine with the ridiculous but inevitable slogan, "You are limited only by your imagination," and architects set about figuring out how to use it. With the new tools of customization, this cycle can be reversed. Skillful designers, well versed in the craft of building, will find they can create means and methods rather than be encircled by them. Frank Gehry didn't find titanium roof panels in a catalog. His design demanded a new method and material. Collaboration with his supplier, experts in the craft of manipulating their materials, led to the solution.

Ironically, the technology that during the nineteenth and twentieth century interrupted this centuries-old collaboration is in large part facilitating its return. Architects and their craftsmen collaborators are using highly advanced manufacturing technologies to fight back. Like the martial arts expert who uses his opponent's strength against him, contemporary craftsmen are using sophisticated advanced manufacturing techniques to build custom made products in direct competition with more traditional forms. Digital tools and machines, invented to improve factory productivity, can be used to make custom components that outperform their mass-produced cousins. Now, how does one capitalize on this opportunity? What follows are some examples.

Case Study 1:
I See What You Mean
(The Big Blue Bear)

40

Conceptual artist Lawrence Argent was commissioned to provide a large public art piece for the Colorado Convention Center; the project was completed in 2005. His proposal, based on one of his son's toys, was developed by scanning the small bear into a computer using 3D laser scanning and then morphing its shape through the use of computer animation software. The process works more efficiently if the 3D computer shape is reduced to fewer triangles, which coincidentally suited the artist's vision. This pixilated bear was blue because that was the color of the plastic in the rapid prototyping machine at the time—another coincidence that caught on…. It stands nearly forty feet tall and peers into the third-story window at the steady stream of out-of-towners as they invade Denver. The disbelieving bear seems to comment to his fellow citizens: "I see what you mean," giving the sculpture its title. Although possible to build in other materials, the artist in consultation with our team chose to use composites, specifically fiberglass reinforced plastics (FRP) that are typically used for boat building, wind turbines, and myriad industrial and consumer products. They are durable, strong, can be easily molded into complex shapes, and can be engineered to withstand the extremes of Denver's winter cold and the occasional tornado. Furthermore, through the use of a unique flange mating process the joints between the segments fit so tightly they disappear. Also, they reliably index the segments to assure a precise fit and are strong enough to transfer loads through the joints, making the structural system more efficient. Through a series of focused discussions, the potential opportunities of the materials and fabrication process were explored to resolve numerous challenges. Because of open collaboration, the end result became a more faithful representation of Argent's idea than if the artist had attempted to dictate a method. The joints are a good example: instead of specifying from the outset that joints must be one-quarter inch, the entire method was assessed, resulting in joints whose width was zero. It was determined that making them one-quarter inch would have been far more difficult, more time consuming, more costly, as well as less attractive.

1.01 Miniature rapid prototype bear used by artist in his presentation to the client is compared to a CNC milled foam "shop drawing" made by Kreysler & Associates to keep track of the many CNC milled pieces of this sculpture during fabrication. The original data was derived by scanning a toy bear and altering its shape using the computer program Maya. Data was exported to the rapid prototype machine for presentation purposes (blue happened to be the color in the machine at the time) and then sent to the fabricator for fabrication estimating, production design, and engineering.

1.02 Expanded Polystyrene (EPS) foam mold with three fiberglass reinforced plastics (FRP) panels being fabricated. Note the integral assembly flanges that will separate the parts but allow accurate and tight reassembly. This "indexed" joint provides structural integrity and a nearly watertight seam, which in fact can be rendered water–tight by the introduction of an elastomeric sealant before bolting through the flanges.

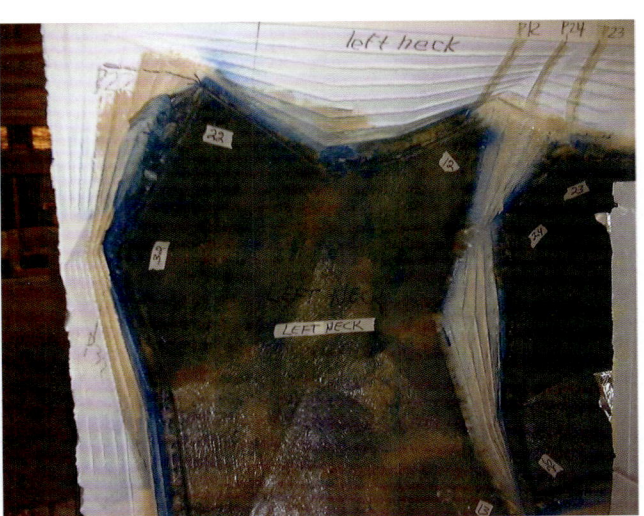

1.03 FRP panel in its mold shows the intricate and complex labeling process facilitated by the ubiquitous masking tape and felt tip marking pen technique. Sometimes the digital way isn't the best way. Note the contour lines in the foam outside the boundary of the mold surface indicating areas not needed as mold surfaces and the blue "overspray" evident around the FRP where the integral color was applied prior to the lay-up of the fiberglass layers. Panels were "nested" to optimize material and CNC milling time.

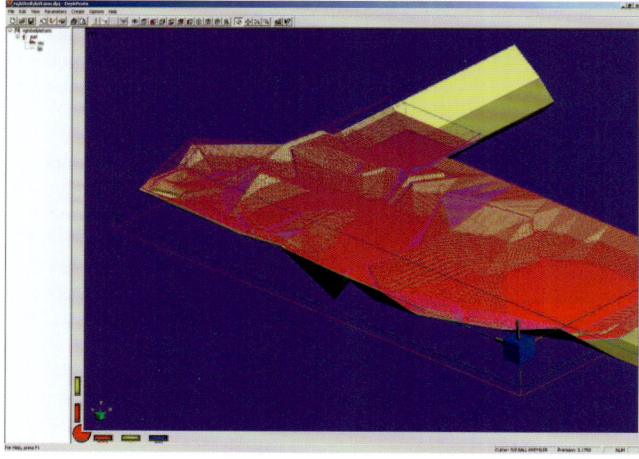

1.04 Computer simulation of a "tool path" is calculated using CAM software. The yellow indicates where the digital craftsman placed foam blocks to best utilize the materials and machine time. Such simulation also helps avoid collisions between materials and equipment during the milling phase. As automated as this process may seem, much is left to the skill of the craftsman driving the design of the manufacturing process.

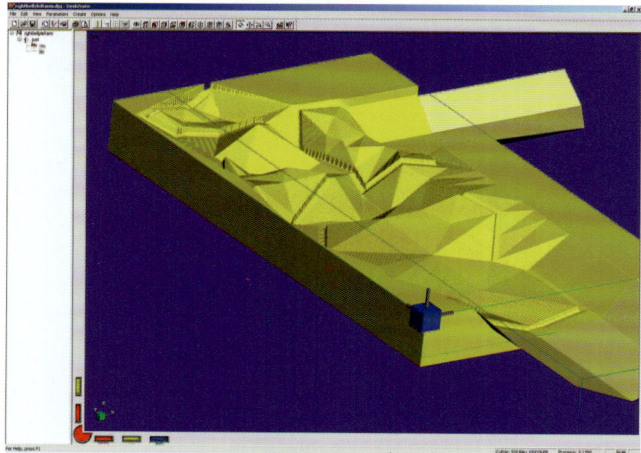

1.05 The final step in preparing the tool path; this shows the operator what the finished mold will look like and how the material will be oriented.

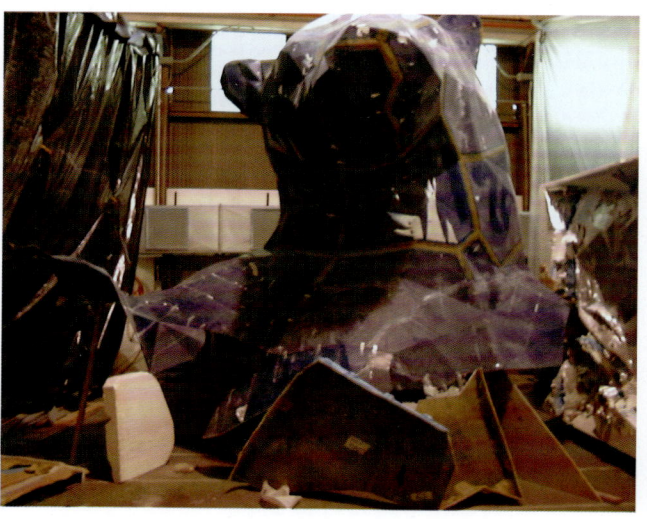

1.06 An assembly of molded FRP panels begins to take final form. Note the uncolored strips where panels have been permanently bonded to one another and the faint but decipherable assembly flanges at the bottom of the assembled parts where the head will be later bolted to the torso. Determination of the size of these assemblies took into account aesthetics and the very practical limitations of shipping.

1.07 This horizontal bulkhead made of fiberglass on two sides of a wood core was a structural component and also served as a work platform during assembly.

1.08 EPS foam, although desirable because it is recyclable and inexpensive, will dissolve when it comes in contact with polyester resin. So, we protect the foam with household tinfoil. This produces an impermeable barrier, which although not ideal for intricate fidelity, is inexpensive. Again, a considerable level of craftsmanship plays an important role in a process that most inexperienced observers might see as highly automated and independent of human factors.

1.09 Color coded diagram generated from the 3D model showing the panelisation of the Big Blue Bear

1.10   "I see what you mean" also known as The Big Blue Bear peers into the third floor of the Colorado Convention Center to inspect the outsiders invading his domain. The sculpture, although it shows no visible joints, is made of six separate parts, shipped on three flatbed trucks and assembled on site over two days. The tight clearance between the bear and the windows required stiffness in the structure most easily and economically accomplished with a partial steel frame. This combination of traditional and contemporary methods is once again where craftsmanship and knowledge of materials plays an important role in the realization of such projects within budget and on schedule.

Case Study 2: Bay House
(A Monocoque Structure)

Another method in design and fabrication is exemplified by Bay House, which overlooks San Francisco Bay and was designed by Miranda Leonard with Walker Moody Architects serving as the local architects of record. This project unites all of the most current tools of the digital age, including laser scanning, finite element analysis engineering, CNC milling and advanced composite materials to realize a building with no frame, a shape with no corners, and a form which started as a physical model inspired by the landscape where it was to be built. Unlike some freeform shapes, this one uses its skin for strength, thus it is a true monocoque structure with a structural skin, like a seed pod or shell. Leonard's design was not inspired by a specific technology; indeed, much of it was barely available when she first imagined this house over fifteen years ago. Instead she used one fundamental tool to great advantage: she was open to collaboration with craftsmen. Her plaster model was laser scanned to provide a 3D digital model for the fabrication and engineering teams. This model became the basis of the FEA engineering and untimately the mold fabrication for the building panels. While Buckminster Fuller's Fly Eye Domes of the 1960s embraced and tested the limits of the Industrial Revolution's production techniques, this project looked outside of, and beyond, the industrial toolkit. In this sense the Bay House is more of a revolution than a logical conclusion. For years, designers and talented engineering firms searched for a means and method to build this house but without success. Only after numerous attempts at torturing and manipulating traditional materials and methods were they abandoned in favor of composite materials and the efficient use of skins as their own support structure.

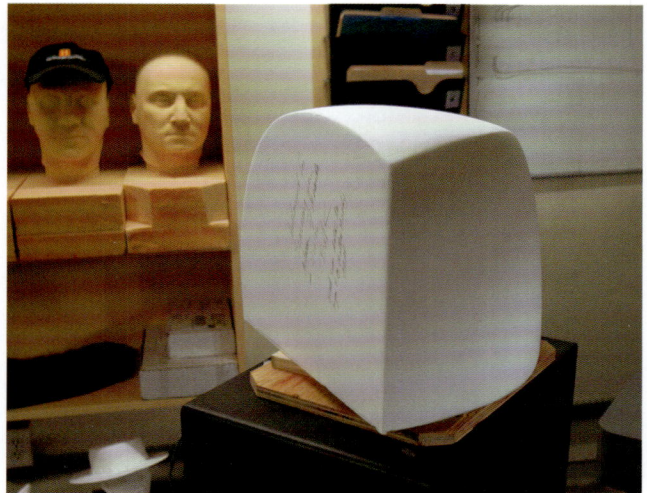

2.01   The designer's original "construction document" was developed as a response to the site topography and modified over several years during the design process with Maya and other 3D tools. The final form, after CAD adjustments were complete, was CNC milled in foam, then a mold and plaster cast were made and hand–sculpted once again. This final form was scanned using Cyberware Laser Detection and Ranging (LADAR) tools for documentation and manufacturing.

[Note, the George Washington heads in the background were milled as part of a research project funded by the George Washington Museum, Mount Vernon, to digitally reconstruct the younger man based on forensic anthropological conjecture. Heads are not part of the exhibit at the George Washington Museum.]

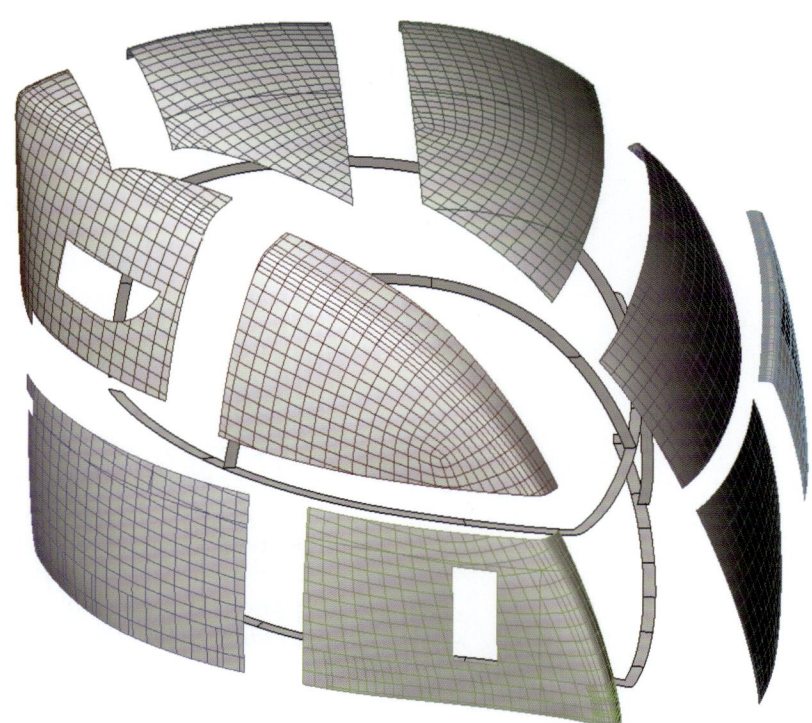

2.02   Rhino model of Bay House is ready to be sent to the architect for construction documentation and to the digital fabricator for mold–making. Horizontal rings represent the foundation and first floor support flange to be integrally molded out of FRP. Window and door openings are also integrally molded into the monocoque shell.

2.03   Building skin is subjected to load testing to verify finite element results. Composite design, because of its extremely high strength, is typically governed by deflection, and allowable deflections are frequently met before the materials undergo even a fraction of allowable stress. This provides an opportunity for well–trained architects to optimize their design for better strength and stiffness to create a smarter and more efficient use of materials.

2.04   One of nine molds used to create the building shell is nearing completion in the large gantry. This three–axis machine has been in operation in various forms since 1990 and has been used to make such diverse projects as Robert Graham's sculpture of Duke Ellington in Central Park, Claes Oldenburg and Coosje van Bruggen's Cupid's Span in San Francisco and aquarium tanks for Monterey Bay Aquarium. It will be replaced in 2010 by a 65 ft x 25 ft x 10 ft five-axis mill as we prepare for even more digitally intensive architecture.

2.05   Pre-assembly of Bay House at our facility in Napa allowed us to verify the assembly and cure the posts to remove the odor of styrene. We also verified our center of gravity (CG) calculations for safe and accurate handling. Once again, craftsmanship plays an important role to efficiently execute these seemingly automated processes.

2.06   The two-inch sandwich construction provided some insulation. However, we found that it was unnecessary to make the balsa core to be placed between the two three–sixteenth–inch fiberglass skins more than two inches. It was not needed for structure and too costly solely for insulation purposes. Also, ventilation, electrical, and fire suppression equipment needed to be included so custom FRP standoff brackets were fabricated and epoxy bonded to the interior skin. Wood battens were installed in preparation to make a lath substructure and the final marmolino plaster finish. This nearly forgotten craft is experiencing a renaissance as architects continue to explore shapes whose surfaces are not easily made with traditional sheet rock or panels.

2.07 A   Contrary to common perception, building codes are not necessarily the enemy of new materials and methods. This excerpt from a fire test report to verify that the material complied with fire codes shows that codes do have means and methods for evaluating new materials.

2.07 B   Unfortunately, too often fabricators or architects assume a material will not pass and do not even try to use it, or worse they try to slip by without being noticed. Knowledge of materials, manufacturing techniques, and design are not quite enough. Fabricators and architects need to understand how their materials can and should be used and importantly, how to navigate through the approval process.

2.08   Bay House sits nestled on the side of a hill, over-
        looking San Francisco Bay. Brisk westerly winds,
        salt laden air, sometimes violent Pacific storms in
        winter, and frequent foggy summer afternoons
        are no match for this durable composite two-
        story main structure. Photo © 2009 Mark Darley

Case Study 3: Translucent Composite Lantern

Greg Lynn's Bloom House in Santa Monica, includes a serpentine lighting element fastened to the ceiling and illuminated from within. Although this is a complex form, the biggest challenge was the decision by the building code official to require this form meet very stringent fire code requirements. Although a Type IV building, it was decided that the lighting element must be made of a Class I material as defined by the ASTM E-84 tunnel test. Plexiglas or other thermoplastics were out of the question. Fiberglass reinforced polymers could possibly meet these requirements but had never been built as a translucent element. Usually fire retardant resins derive their properties from fillers that render the resin opaque. Lynn worked with us to research different combinations of materials. A great deal of new work is being done in this area, and we had the enthusiastic support of materials labs, academics, and code consultants. Ultimately, we incorporated new technology in the form of translucent intumescent materials. Intumescence is a fire-resistant technique that relies on a material's tendency to build a protective layer of carbon char, like a marshmallow in a campfire, to protect the material beneath. At the same time that this decision was made, the fabrication of mold making, engineering, and installation coordination was proceeding. The "construction document" was a 3D computer model that we imported and then segmented into pieces, which were both moldable and manageable for installation and maintenance purposes. Using our large-format CNC gantry router, we milled a mold directly. This avoided the cost of an extra step to make a pattern and the extra layer of construction tolerances for error. All fabrication processes have inherent tolerances; tight tolerances cost more than loose ones. Perhaps the best way to minimize "tolerance creep" resulting from multiple steps in a process is to avoid extra steps. By going directly to a mold, rather than a pattern, we avoided the inherent error, which would have been derived by manufacturing a mold. Although small, these errors accumulate and can result in undesirable design compromises. Also because Lynn allowed wider tolerances at the assembly joints, it was possible to mill the molds without having to fabricate the intimate mating flanges used in the Blue Bear, for example. The project exemplified the designer's skillful use of materials and fabrication techniques in the complex world of construction in which building codes, materials, manufacturing systems, and coordination between trades must all work in tandem.

In sum, it must be recognized that new ideas and tools creep into use. The first iron chisel did not replace stone overnight. Band saws were around for a long time before they replaced circular saws in lumber mills. So it will be with 3D tools and machines and advanced materials. Some people will insist their time is decades away while others will use them tomorrow. Indeed, many of these techniques and materials have been around for years. Above are only a very few recent examples. Zaha Hadid used translucent FRP sandwich panels on Mind Zone in 1999. The entire Silver Legacy casino dome in Reno, Nevada, was built without the use of steel or lumber but made entirely out of FRP sandwich panels in the 1980s. Digital fabrication tools and advanced materials have been in common use in architecture for decades. However, it is only recently that software and CNC tool costs have become affordable enough that architects can begin to explore the vast potential these tools offer on a large scale. Buildings can be hung, not held up from the ground. Walls can support themselves without frames and bracing, in the same way that nature builds structural systems. Window mullions, sills, door jambs, electrical outlets and cable raceways can be integral parts of a wall system containing in one piece the hundreds of components found in a typical wall assembly, including its supporting structure. But as these techniques and tools become available, practitioners must recognize that their practice has changed. They must once again as in centuries past, build bridges to the means and methods of making things differently than we have for the last 150 years—both by honing their skills and by building alliances with craftsmen. To make these new tools more than a novelty, and instead to become vehicles to make things well, efficiently, environmentally sustainable, and economically, it will require designers who understand their new role and who nurture new partnerships with the men and women who practice the crafts needed to make them happen. Only then will the true value of these new materials and the tools we use to design and fabricate them be realized.

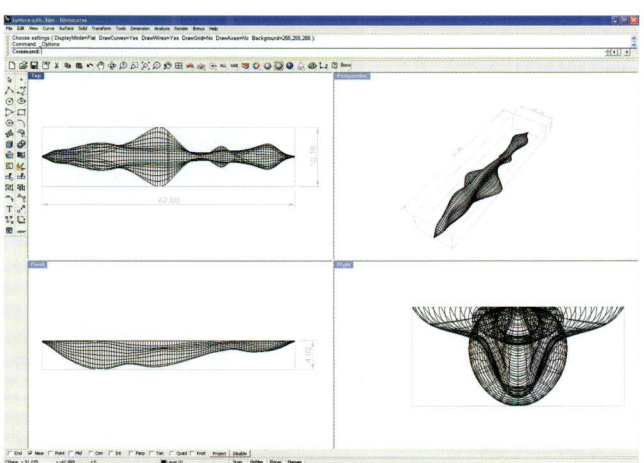

3.01   The architect's 3D Maya file is imported into Rhino for estimating. 3D data is not only essential for CNC manufacturing but is equally valuable for producing cost estimates. Factors that influence cost including surface area, volume, milling time, and overall fabrication strategy are quickly and easily derived from 3D data.

51

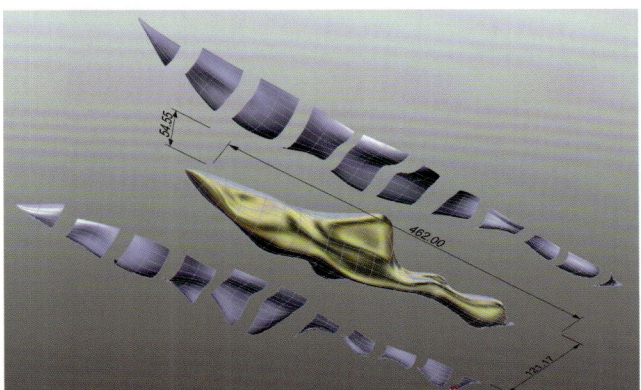

3.02   Manufacturing strategy is developed and modeled for the architect's review and approval. This rendering shows the panelization strategy based on material, installation, and maintenance constraints. Although FRP composites can be fabricated in virtually any size, handling or the dimension of a door opening will control the size. Here, the digital craftsman helps the design team visualize the process and evaluate the strategy.

3.03 Once the panelization strategy and fabrication design is approved, the mold–making process begins. Similar to Bay House and the Blue Bear, molds are CNC milled out of recyclable EPS foam and protected with foil. Here certified composites technician and craftsman Miguel Ambriz applies foil to the mold surface. Since individual panels needed to be removable at random for maintenance, locking flanges were not appropriate. Although the flanges that were used do not fit as tightly, they allow for easy removal. Products made by computer can be fabricated to high tolerances. However things like thermal expansion and contraction, material stresses, manufacturing tolerances, material shrinkage, and tool error play a huge role in determining cost. The design that depends on tight tolerances will be more expensive, often many times more expensive, than one benefiting from the knowledge and skill of a designer who understands and allows for reasonable tolerances.

3.04 Translucent FRP requires special care. Here the recently fabricated and uncured panels are covered with plastic sheet to avoid dust or dirt from settling on the laminate before final curing. Meanwhile, the mold in the foreground is coated with clear resin and ready for fiberglass layers to be applied.

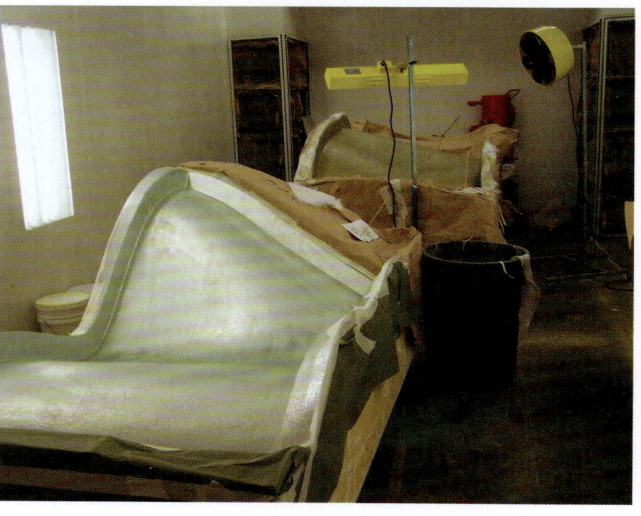

3.05 After the flange has been cured initially and wet trimming is complete, the mold and its part are moved to the oven for the post cure process. This drives off residual styrene odor and improves dimensional stability and fire resistance. These panels were required to meet ASTM E-84 Class 1 flame spread and smoke performance, which initiated a research and design effort to devise such high fire resistance while retaining maximum translucency. Material suppliers were instrumental in resolving this unique problem along with the help of Professor Nick Dembsey of Worchester Polytechnic Institute, Worchester, MA, who is an expert in the use of composites for construction applications.

3.06   Lantern is pictured after installation at the Bloom
        House in Santa Monica. Note the importance of
        careful coordination between the architect and
        the fabricator to determine the proper joint loca-
        tion. Translucent FRP has been chosen for this
        project specifically because it is not transparent.
        So overlaps, thick spots versus thin and anchors
        all have important visual impacts.

Lorenzo Marasso
Gabrielle Ho
Ashima Chitre

Case Studies

Folds, Bodies, and *Boats*
Lorenzo Marasso

Folds, Bodies, and *Boats* reconsiders form in the age of computer technology and advanced fabrication techniques. Building form is traditionally understood from the assembly of discrete building components. Today, digital variability made possible through CNC machines disengages form from the economy of repetition and makes smooth, curvilinear composite structures feasible. We may consider form to be a composite whole and no longer the sum of parts.

With this in mind, further exploration into structure provokes a contemporary reinterpretation of the concept of load bearing. Although it is still constrained to Euclidian geometries, Borromini's cupola of San Carlo alle Quatro Fontane in Rome was considered "heretic" in its day. This particular cupola painstakingly resolved a very complicated set of conditions using the available technologies, albeit in configurations the general public found unsettling. The twenty-first century not only creates new complexities and problems, but also new technologies and solutions. As it was for Borromini in his time, pushing contemporary technological limits requires a general reconsideration of what we expect from a building.

Folds, Bodies, and *Boats* proposes a system of bespoke structural bearing panels that efficiently and beautifully address the challenges and ambitions of the building. Because of the radical sculptural form, the load distribution does not follow traditional computational and structural rationale. As a result of computing the forces at play, the panel design adapts to become thinner where forces are the least and vice-versa. The Voronoi pattern further enhances the panel performance as it develops a load distribution that mimics structures found in nature, like the wings of a dragonfly. Natural systems utilize a complex and active structural logic that properly suits the design and fabrication tools at our fingertips today.

Interior view of major structural elements and skin

Exterior view of skinned volume at water's edge

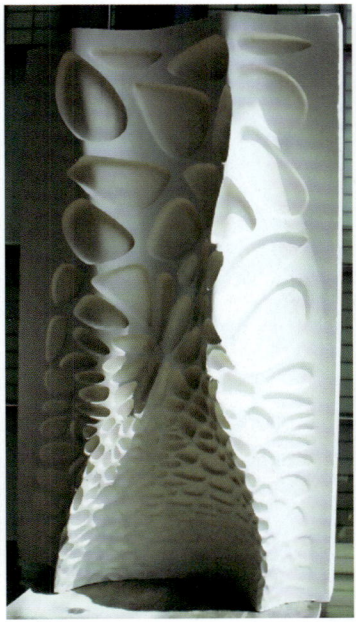

This panel mock-up, developed with Lasha Brown shows the structurally efficient Voronoi pattern.

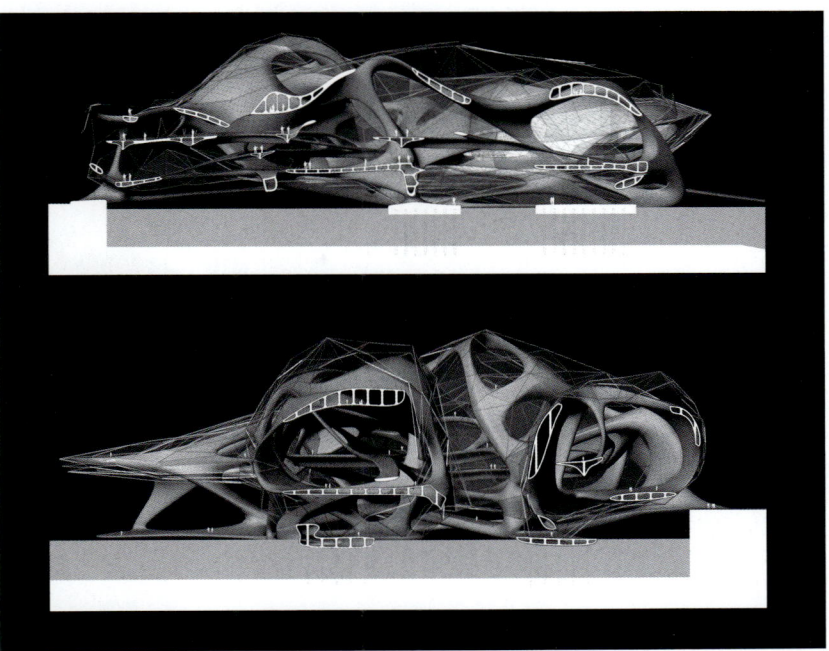

Architectural section showing inhabitable structural bones and programmed interstitial voids between structure and skin

Structural study model

Covered launch area for boat debut

View of factory from water

Carbon Weave
Gabrielle Ho

Beautiful, high performance sailboats are built of exotic lightweight materials and designed using state-of-the-art surface modeling software. These nautical hotrods challenge the architect to compete in the drag race of technology. Building was once the world's most innovative industry in design, engineering, industrialization, and material use. Automobiles chased the building industry at the turn of the twentieth century. The Sears' craftsman houses, for example, were far more advanced in their design, sales, shipping, construction, advertising, and manufacture than the Model T. Fifty years later, the aerospace industry overtook the others to become the leader in materials and design.

Today, competitive yachting is among the most advanced, high performance, design-led industries. The merger between design, material research, testing, and unprecedented funding makes offshore race boats and their recreational cousins the apex of the synthesis of high performance, exotic materials, and beauty today. It is this constant conversation between design and materials that drives such tremendous innovation. The focus on the design of surfaces and their specific quality makes this industry a great partner for architectural design.

Carbon Weave stands at the cusp of the practical world of manufacturing and the glamorous world of race boats, showcasing its material of choice: carbon fiber. The roof employs the logic and evokes the characteristics of carbon fiber construction. While it is flat to allow for flexible machinery configurations, it is made intricate by imitating the weave of carbon fiber. At an architectural scale, the weave creates a compelling visual effect by manipulating light with its multi-directional reflective properties. The strands that make up the roof's structure drape down into the open space as program dictates. Vertical surfaces are angled to specifically address the reflections of sky and water. Moreover, the maneuver accentuates the impossible thinness of the roof. The result is a building that stays true to its function as a manufacturing shed while showcasing the technological wonders of race boats.

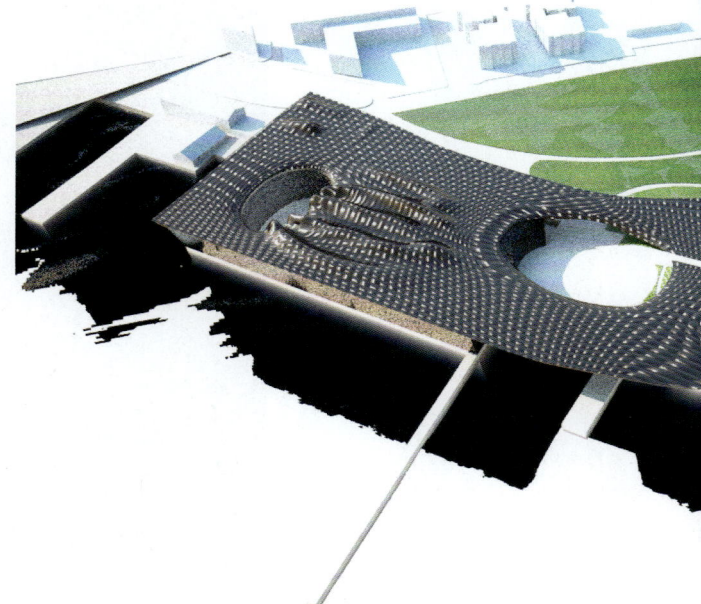

Bird's eye view of site showing adjacent Gas Works Park

58

Model showing factory floor and glazing system

Rendered elevation of factory from park approach

View of yacht factory from water

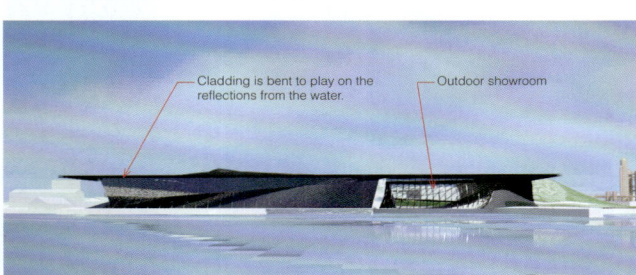

Cladding is bent to play on the reflections from the water.

Outdoor showroom

Rendered elevation of factory showing razor thin woven roof structure

Model showing building facade at water's edge

Composite Canopies
Ashima Chitre

A forest of vertical spires collides in a shimmering canopy. The web of structure and translucent skin which compose this canopy grows from robust trunks floating above and enclosing the understory. The "stems" gradually merge with the ground plane. Each "mushroom" of the canopy proves to be exceptionally beneficial to the program of a boat factory, where long spans and wide open spaces are required to maneuver the boats through each stage of manufacturing. Because 3DL sail manufacturers and hull fabricators build their own five- and three-axis mills and gantries, it is no hindrance to reconfigure their linear arrangements into a radial logic. The gantries are carved into the undersides of five of the larger mushroom "caps." These nodes serve to organize the remaining program, integrating specific function into the structure of the building and allowing for ultimate flexibility in the rest of the space.

The canopies cluster to create a structural framework. The cellular nature of the system allows for specific control over natural light. Not unlike a typical factory where temporary walls and plastic curtains delineate function, smaller spaces are defined as needed for offices, autoclave ovens, and cold storage facilities. The color of the canopy is determined by the color of the composite Kevlar fabric used for high-tech sails on racing vessels. While the fabric is used sparingly for sails to cut weight and enhance performance, this project uses multiple layers of Kevlar to create a tight richly golden weave of composite fibers. It is the nature of composites that through adjustments to the lamination thickness, a material that is ideal for one purpose might find life in another. In this instance the Kevlar is used liberally as a composite with steel to support the heavy gantries.

The site provides three different states for the building to respond to: the shoreline, the hillside, and the urban fabric. The stems work particularly well as they negotiate a relationship to the shore—marching out to bring water access to the gantries. The canopy lightly mingles with the hillside, and the raised slab creates a sidewalk to accept the urban fabric. The project responds dexterously to

site and function through a composite logic. A straightforward strategy with simple materials is intricately laminated to provide intelligent solutions.

Interior model view of sail loft with Radial 3DL machine.

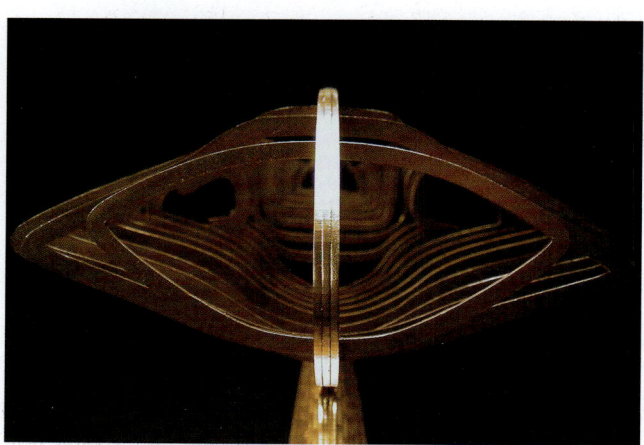

Bulkhead structural study model

Interior model view of hull manufacturing with radial CNC Mill

Varying height of stretched skin aramid canopy allow the passage of light and provide greater depth as structurally necessary.

Elevation of factory showing vertical emphasis to core columns and simple skin at perimeter

Architectural plan and section of yacht factory

Surfaces

Between buildings, boats, automobiles, graphics, and fashion, the word surface has innumerable shades of meaning. To achieve their idea of a perfect surface, transportation designers have sculpted smooth, glossy car bodies into scores of sexy riffs on the automobile. Boat designers have honed the hulls of their boats to achieve fantastic fluid dynamic performance. Architects have bent building systems—like sheet goods and two-by-fours—into at times tortured structures to support the curvatures of their expression. In graphic design the surface is the contemporary canvas, be it the side of a bus, road sign, book cover, or web page. Fashion has used surface as the superficial, the facade, even as illusion. The common ground of all of these meandering redefinitions is that surface is a mediator between two distinct things. It is the vehicle through which the eye perceives a form, the way a solid meets a fluid, or the way a concept meets an audience.

This section follows the explorations of three distinct designers who, throughout their careers have wrestled with the concept of surface. What happens when a magazine no longer has a cover, and is not printed on paper? What if a car body isn't smooth and reflective and what else can its shell say about its contents besides "car?" How do details provide a design with depth, and what is the difference between car and boat design?

Greg Foley has collaborated with designers of perfume, toys, packaging, and countless others in his work with the boundary challenging *Visionaire* magazine. In this, as with all of his work, he has proven the richness of cross-media exchange of ideas. The following piece investigates a means of evaluating and developing his hard-to-define creations.

Chris Bangle, one of the decade's most intriguing and controversial transportation designers, considers the varying definitions of surface. The auto industry is loosening its grip on the idea of the "perfect" surface, while other disciplines are just grasping the technology and acumen to work with it. Across industries, designers are trading trends and tools to find a new way to visualize and even build their work.

Adriana Monk writes on the challenges of designing objects in motion and the advantages of working between various modes of transportation. She constantly searches for a harmony between exterior expression and interior detailing, taking cues from boat and car surfaces for the details that unify a design.

The following pages illuminate the paths that designers have taken in trying to look more deeply into the surfaces they were trained to manicure so obsessively. When they look past the polish and into the depths, improbable outcomes, imperfections, and new expressions lie beneath the surface.

Surfaces

Greg Foley

Elemental Story: Why & How

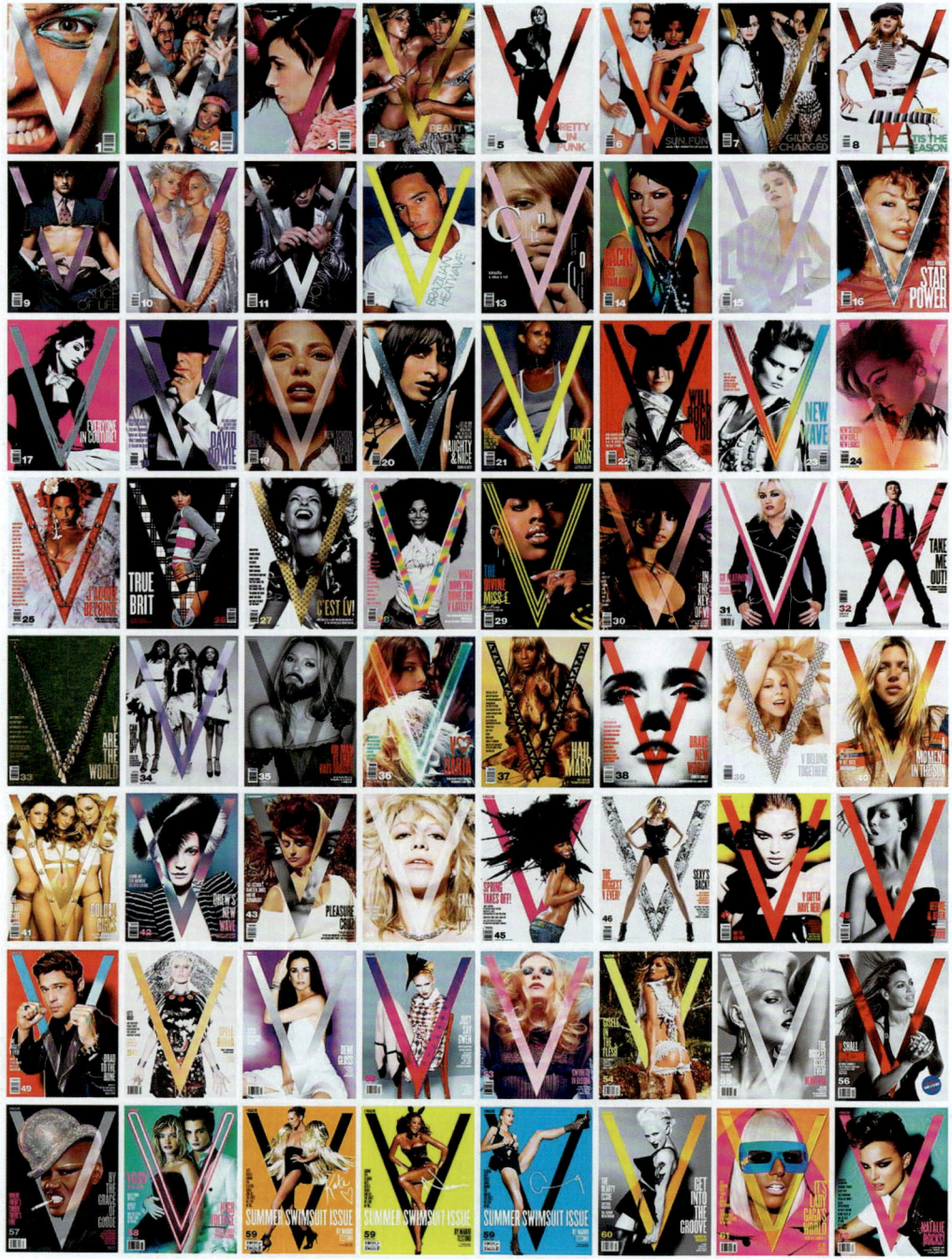

V Magazine, issues V1 (1999)–V62 (2010)

SPRING, SUMMER, EROTICA, HEAVEN, FUTURE, SEA, BLACK, ORIENT, FACES, ALPHABET, WHITE, DESIRE, SEVEN DEADLY SINS, HYPE!, CINDERELLA, CALENDAR, GOLD, FASHION, BEAUTY, DIAMOND, CHIC, LIGHT, FANTASY, MOVEMENT, BIBLE, WOMAN, GAME, BLUE, WHERE?, TOUCH, PARIS, MAN, POWER, MEMOS, LOVE, PLAY, ROSES, WORLD, SCENT, DREAMS, TOYS, MORE TOYS, UNCENSORED, TASTE, MAGIC, DECADES, HARMONY, PRIVATE, SOUND, SPORT, SURPRISE, SOLAR, 2010.

What do you see here and how should this be read? In this case, it could be simply a list of titles and themes for a quarterly publication called *Visionaire*. But these words provide potent clues, each pointing in an alternate direction. Collected together, they reflect an editorial process and sensibility. Organized chronologically, they are the building blocks of the publication's history. To a knowledgeable reader, the simple list becomes an analogical library of almost two decades of *Visionaire* issues.

Visionaire represents a cross section of contemporary design concerns. As a periodic publication, it challenges our understanding of both form and content. Each issue is organized around a theme, which is elucidated through new production techniques and technologies. Contributors from a wide range of creative disciplines participate without typical commercial constraints, and often a relationship with an appropriate sponsor is formed in order to fully realize the potential of a specific issue.

Successful design often appears to be self-evident. However, a designer's choice of material, composition, and surface detail can also leave a viewer asking "why?" My projects in a variety of media including the publications *Visionaire*, its siblings *V Magazine* and *VMAN*, luxury and mainstream branding, product design, music and video direction, books, catalogues, exhibitions, events, a course at Parsons School of Design, and a number of popular children's book series, gives me a broad perspective on creative culture. Regardless of the project, the notion of "story" provides orientation. In terms of design, this addresses the questions of "why" and "how" a finished product looks the way it does.

First, what is story, and is it the same thing as narrative? Not necessarily. The story that interests me here is the generative endeavor. This differs from narrative that, like a design, is the vehicle for a process. In practical terms, story may be the needs, ideas, or data that drive and inform a project's development. Narrative is the decisive pattern that organizes and conveys them. To confuse a design with its underlying principle is like confusing a metaphor with the meaning it expresses. Similarly, style and content, effect and relevance, idealization and identity must hang in balance. Design and narrative both rely on the elemental tools of story, which can shape better decisions about the smallest detail.

There are several ways that *Visionaire* exhibits story. Often a production technique or new technology catalyzes the theme and the issue's title becomes shorthand for it. Discoveries about the theme are contextualized and related from a specific point of view. Once it gets refined and communicated the story is immediately activated in the hands of the reader. Informing all of this is *Visionaire's* identity as a periodic publication, which is expected to be both consistent and innovative.

In VISIONAIRE 42. SCENT the goal was to create a series of original fragrances, each inspired and represented by an image. For years, we wanted to connect with all five of the viewer's senses directly through the format of publishing. Here was an opportunity for our contributing artists, designers, and writers to collaborate with the most highly regarded perfumers at International Flavors and Fragrances

(IFF). The perfumers were invited to create challenging scents, not subject to client conventions or "dumbing down" for the mass market. It was the practice of these "Noses" that became our core story—beginning with the liquid.

Rather than apply "dry" fragrance to a printed page, we featured the "juice" in spray vials arranged by number like a guessing game. Inside the issue there were acid-free blotter sticks and a booklet of imagery with corresponding numbers. The overall packaging was based on small cases that a Nose brings to present modifications to clients. Because the liquid (in muted colors) was the primary focus, the materials used for the case, book, and blotters served as a background of varying textures in white.

The scents included: *Hunger* by Karl Lagerfeld (perfumer Sandrine Malin) recalls buttery baked bread, *Success* by David Bowie (Christophe Laudamiel) evokes sexy dirty money, *Fear* by Stephen King (Pierre Wargnye and Braja Mookherjee) captures the essence of living mimosa flowers, *Space* by Zaha Hadid (Sophie Labbe) was purposely abstract.

Because the SCENT issue was so well received by our audience, contributors, and (especially for our collaborative sponsor) in the media, we were asked by IFF to revisit their labs and develop a complementary issue, VISIONAIRE 47. TASTE. For us, this was another of the five senses we hadn't explored. We learned that although approximately 75% of flavor is scent, an effective flavor relies on being identifiable. In other words, it cannot be abstract. Consequently, there are Noses who engineer flavor, but fewer "Flavorists" who also create fragrances—so we had a new team.

With flavor as the story, the viewer was actively invited to identify a familiar sensation through an unfamiliar medium. We didn't want to feature liquid again after the SCENT issue, so the Flavorists created fast dissolve tablets. But the natural reaction was to spit them out after a few seconds of tasting. Eventually we located a gel tab plant willing to work on our limited run. The typical tastes they manufacture are mint, cinnamon, or citrus. Our issue featured flavors such as: pine nuts, condensed milk, spray adhesive, earth, sweat, jet fuel, eggs, chips, and two kinds of chocolate—mixed with

leather or truffle. The gel tab technology melted on the tongue—committing the participant to the experience. However, it was a challenge to stabilize the array of flavors on the dry medium (in particular, the subtleties of egg).

For the packaging, we built onto the story of the scent issue, but subverted its look by substituting equal opposites. Instead of vials, we arranged gel packs. We were able to flip the arrangement to feature the gel tabs on the inside of the cover because gel medium is lighter than paper, and we created a heavier board-style book which acted as a base. The images were reduced to icons in lieu of number coding. What was soft, matte, and white for the scent isse became luscious, glossy, and black for TASTE.

The final sense we had not dealt with directly was audio. VISIONAIRE 53. SOUND was our opportunity to approach musicians, conceptual artists, and iconic celebrities for contributions. Like all issues of *Visionaire,* it was important that SOUND contained everything the reader/listener would need to enjoy the experience. We decided to present both sound and image by pressing twelve-inch vinyl picture discs—classic for vinyl enthusiasts. But we did not want to house them in a standard portable record player. When the notion of including a "Vinyl Killer" came up during our weekly brainstorm sessions, the package became clear.

A Vinyl Killer is a toy-sized VW Bus that literally drives along the grooves of a record while playing its tracks through a small, integrated speaker. We approached the Japanese company that invented them, and convinced them to make the first custom version of their product as a Mini Cooper—our sponsor for the sound issue. The story was complete.

Visionaire issues that are limited to the senses of sight and touch often use processes and technology to re-imagine the ink medium and encourage the viewer to interact more with the contents. In VISIONAIRE 43. DREAMS we presented inkless images by laser cutting each artwork so that they were revealed only when held up to the light. The ink was used instead to create a "blank" book printed with a continuous, reflective spectrum that housed all the laser cuts. Our production typically pushes the limits of what can be achieved within time and cost restrictions. The constraints of laser cutting informed the dot size matrices we applied

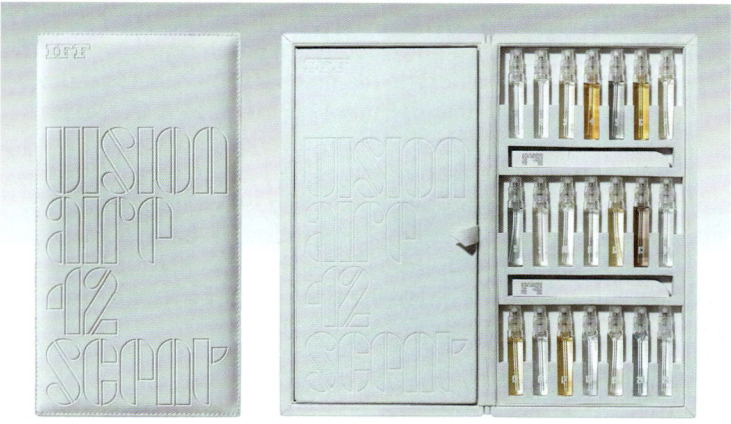

Visionaire 42 Scent (2003), case and interior

Visionaire 43 Dreams (2004), slipcase

Visionaire 47 Taste (2005), case and interior

Visionaire 43 Dreams (2004), lasercut page

Visionaire 53 Sound (2007), case

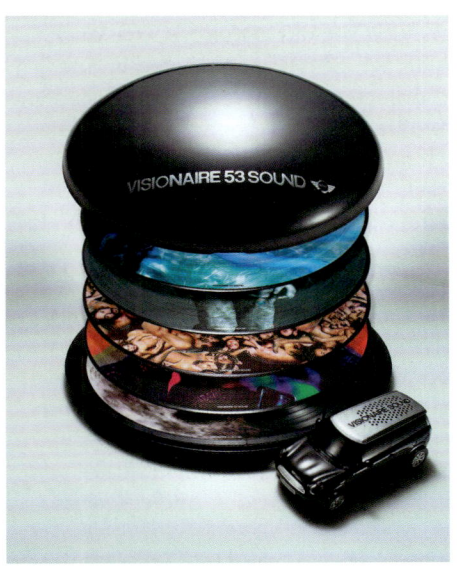

Visionaire 53 Sound (2007), components

to the artworks. Also, the schedule was determined by the maximum number of available lasers working at full capacity, which produced in the end, 22,500 individually cut images.

VISIONAIRE 56. SOLAR implemented a specialized light-sensitive pigment, which becomes chromatic only in direct sunlight, requiring the viewer to take the issue outside. The slipcase uses the same pigment embedded in solid sheet plastic and the book cover features a life-size embroidery (a bird in flight) using light-sensitive thread. Although colorless at first glimpse, when exposed to sunlight, the solar issue bursts into full color.

VISIONAIRE 39. PLAY, VISIONAIRE 48. MAGIC and VISIONAIRE 55. SURPRISE each study moving imagery by using different historic print techniques. In PLAY, we produced a series of flipbooks, and MAGIC contained a stack of transparent lens-like plates. Each artist in these issues was able to feature approximately two seconds of film, video, or animation—more action than any still image can capture. In SURPRISE, we worked closely with a paper engineer to create a series of photographic pop-ups housed in a case that rises toward the viewer when opened. For each of these issues we aimed to improve and contemporize print technologies, which are dynamic but fairly traditional.

While considering what constitutes print and periodic publishing, we also explore what can become a page. For VISIONAIRE 44. TOYS, 45. VISIONAIRE MORE TOYS, and VISIONAIRE 54. SPORT, we printed imagery onto solid objects and knit fabric respectively. At the time, the kidult toy phenomenon was primarily focused on works by graphic and graffiti artists. For our toy issues, we invited twenty of the biggest names in high fashion to design characters onto our own unique figurine. In contrast, the sport issue (co-produced by Lacoste) focuses on the iconic tennis shirt invented by Rene Lacoste, re-imagining it as a blank page. Using inkjet textile printing, we presented full-color photographic panoramas around each garment. The series of shirts were presented in a paginated format that seal with a handle, doubling as a book and a suitcase.

The same tools of story used to develop *Visionaire*, shaped *Thank You Bear*, the first

in a series of children's picture books that I created (intended for children aged two years and older). In the first book, Bear finds a box that reminds him of his friend Mouse. On the way to find Mouse, a series of other animals share their opinions and make Bear doubt his instincts. Eventually, Mouse wanders by and asks Bear what he has found. Bear tentatively shows his friend what he's found and Mouse crawls inside the box declaring it "the greatest thing ever."

The words, illustrations, and overall design of *Thank You Bear* are informed by the ethics of its main character. The notion of character is the active element, which plays out multiple scenarios that become narratives. In the same way that Bear finds inert things and makes good use of them, the book's palette is based on sun-faded samples of construction paper. These colors represent animals within the narrative and are placed as a color code on the book's spine in order of appearance. The book is now being published in nine languages as an ongoing series with three other titles: *Don't Worry Bear, Good Luck Bear,* and *I Miss You Mouse.* The success of the series has afforded that each first edition is printed on environmentally friendly stock (certified by the Forest Stewardship Council), and licensed products are made specially to appear as if they've been found in the woods—so that the consumer may "see" through Bear's eyes.

If story helps the active process of creation become smarter and potentially faster, it is also an effective way to evaluate the result. In this way, story and narrative can divide into active and passive modes. In the active state, a designer seeks threads that link back to the elemental story. Furthermore, the active is the motivating force, the theme, or the central question; it is the intuitive and critical assessment that serves both the needs of the project and the designer's creative point of view. The closer a project gets to realization, the more its active story naturally settles into narrative. The first creative threads, now followed by others, are open to interpretation, criticism, idealization, and repetition. The question "why" relates more to the active, creative state and "how" to the passive, observational, and critical.

Greg Foley

Surfaces

Visionaire 56 Solar (2009), cover embroidery

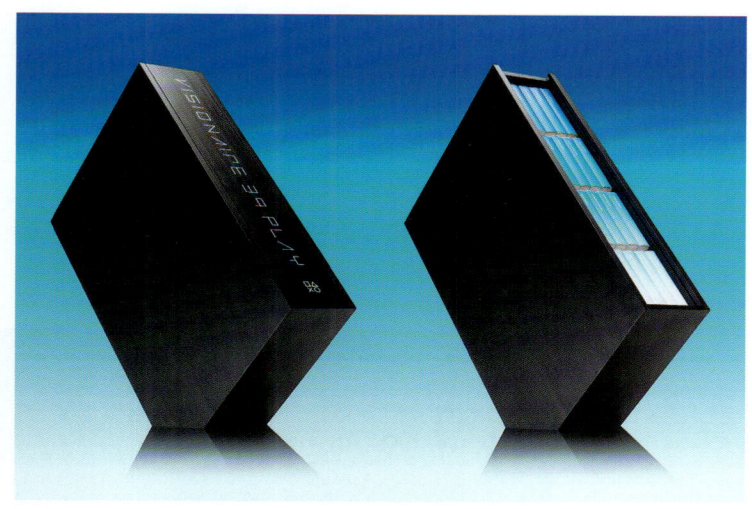

Visionaire 39 Play (2002), wooden case and flipbooks

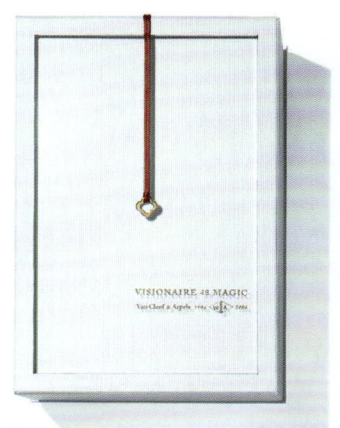

Visionaire 48 Magic (2006), case with Van Cleef & Arpels gold Alhambra

Visionaire 48 Magic (2006), lenticular plates

Visionaire 44 Toys (2004) & 45 More Toys (2005)

Visionaire 55 Surprise (2008), open case and pop-ups

Visionaire 54 Sport (2008), interior Set 2

Thank You Bear (Viking 2007)

Chris Bangle

New Thoughts on Architecture and Car Design

Over the past few years, I have been watching a progression in conceptual architecture regarding idea of surface. I believed that only car designers knew the "true" path towards understanding "perfect surface." I had hoped architects would join in a dialogue with car designers to promote the cause of a holistic cultural aesthetic that could span two major creative media.

Although few architects have transfered concepts of "perfect surfacing" from the car designers to buildings successfully, the reverse has begun to happen—car designers have begun fascinating experiments in non-traditonal car forms and surfaces inspired by conceptual architecture. They have even made their first attempts at non-consistent, irrational, or "imperfect" surfacing. The once clear distinction between what is structure and what is surface has given way to more stylized exploration of surface as structure. At BMW, a fractal approach to surface has been energized by new understandings of vortex generation and flat-plane aerodynamics, much of its lessons learned in the Formula One wind tunnels. In short, not everything must have a soft shape to have good aerodynamics, and sometimes a faceted surface is a better way to control the drag and the downforce on a moving vehicle. While these are experiments in functional geometries they are inspired and guided by an enthusiastic new look at the principles of automotive aesthetics.

More intriguing than improved aerodynamics are the potential weight savings that "imperfect" surfaces can bring: by creating a part of their rigidity through creases and folds their stiffness can be maintained even as they are manufactured in thinner (and thus lighter) sheets. The smaller, tessellated patterns of the flat planes also break the light differently and offer some promise of achieving car manufacturing's Holy Grail: appealing shiny beauty without the factory paint line. One test model developed when I was with BMW Design featured traditional surfacing on the passenger's side and faceted surfaces on the driver's side. Surprisingly the traditional curved surfaces appeared much duller and less refined than the faceted ones even though they were all painted in the same matte silver color. If such an aesthetic became preferred by customers there could be real benefits for everyone—

the paint line in a modern car assembly plant is often its largest energy consumer.

To the uninitiated much of this research appears to be fantasy futurisms, or at best to leverage rational improvements to glorify the merely decorative, but the challenge of evolving automotive surfaces goes beyond incorporating the technical innovations mentioned above. One of the main functions of the vehicle's appearance is to motivate the consumer to purchase by serving as a symbol of the values and sense of style shared by an enviable cohort of other drivers. Although most cars are produced with the same means, operate similarly, and look more or less the same (form follows function, even in cars it seems!), people want to feel that their car is not only special but is also the pinnacle of the brand's heritage. The car design process struggles to maintain visual brand identity even as it is forced to leave behind the well known shapes of tradition. A new look of sustainability, known in BMW Group Design as "Susthetics," needs to be created out of these innovative surfaces joining new functional improvements with a fresh interpretation of the brand's identity.

Jay Kim manages to imply a great deal of function in the surface fractalization; energy right into the glass

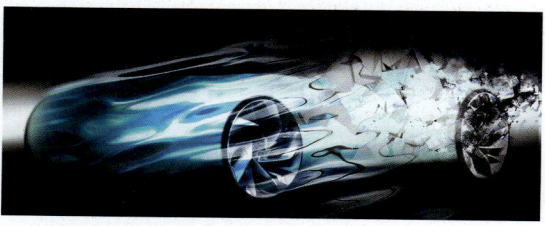

Sweet, inspiring, and just enough undefined to let everyone "solve" the car for themselves. Takumi Yamamoto rendering

Car Form Follows Architecture, as it has been for a century. Dzmitry's homage to Herzog and De Meuron

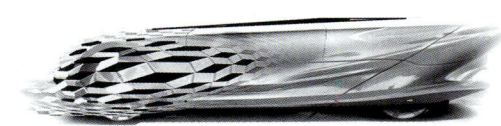

Dzimtry Samal shows 4 themes in a quick sketch approach

Nice emotional "flow" in Raphael Laurent's car, the type of discontinuity that inspires comparison to motorcycle design.

Carl Soares JR. created the first "figurative" car design I have ever seen: a GT40 with wind flowing over, alps passing behind it.

Texture of Form?

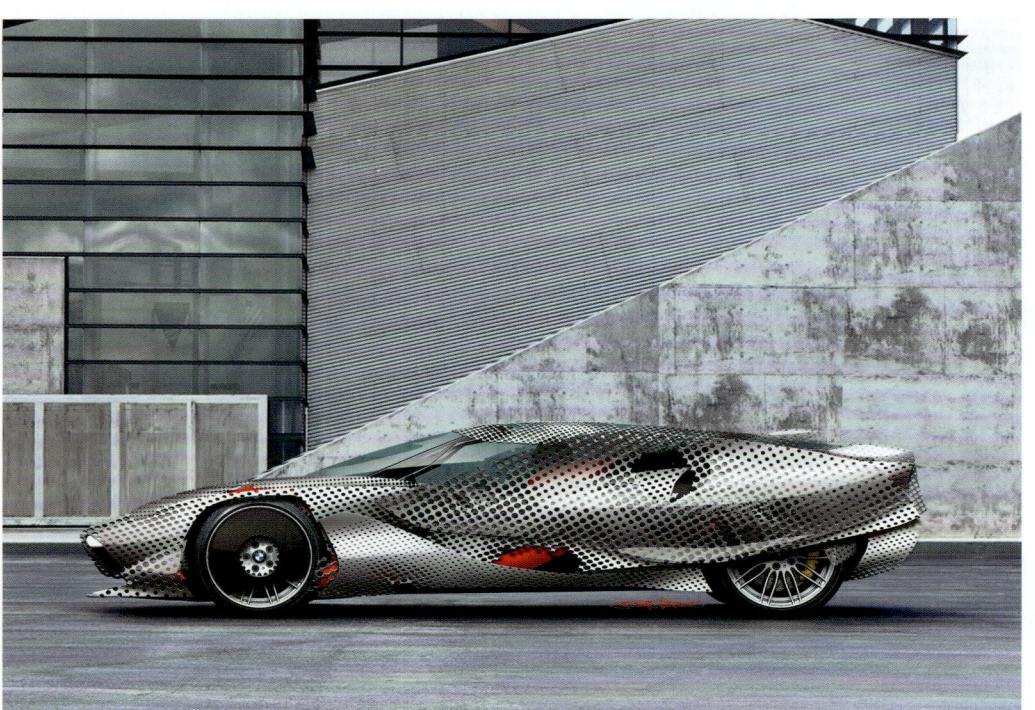

Conceptual studies of potential of perforated surfaces in developing a new, recognizable aesthetic

This is no simple task. A brand's products must be discernable as belonging to a different design paradigm than that of the past if it wishes to be immediately identified with new customer values. In the case of Susthetics, the idea is to make recognizable within the form the often invisible technologies that improve the cars relationship to energy management, driving efficiencies, and the politically correct. These experimental surfaces in car design must be understood as precursors of the visual signals that will set apart super-efficient drive trains of the future from the capabilities of the past.

Today this message is largely communicated through labels and badges on the trunk of the car ("Hybrid," for example) or with a large marketing graphic affixed to the side of a car's body. However, this approach is clearly a stop-gap measure and will prove inadequate when the market becomes saturated with electric and hydrogen vehicles. By then the new breed of vehicles must distinguish itself from its internal combustion kin. People will expect a clear language of values and responsibilities expressed by the shape of the cars in their lives, and car design will need to know how to signal certain identifying clues without resorting to stickers.

The potential for communication does not limit itself to shape. Even car design's basic notions of form and surface will undergo a dramatic re-think when light emmitting capabilities migrate from building facades to cars. It is entirely likely that the passive exterior of the car will give way to an active exterior of digital imaging display panels. The upcoming generation of consumers is far more interested in the user-generated content of social networking than in the sculptural metal forms we car designers have to offer, and when car design embraces the flat facetted surfaces now being experimented with, the marriage of automobile and display facade becomes quite feasible. This could be the Next Big Thing, changing our ideas of personal emotional mobility previously dominated by shiny metal sculptures for eighty years.

While car designers are fashioning a new future for the car from these experiments, contemporary architecture has abandoned the focus on surface altogether, with the exception of the "green facade." Instead, sculpted

Anders Warming (exterior design) at the GINA Light Visionary Model

structure serves as both form and surface without indication that the disciplined handling of light and tonal nuances, reflection continuity, and harmony of curves is a priority, or even desirable.

Instead, predictably, the "brash gesture of the impossible" is the raison d'etre of these buildings, and admittedly they are exciting. Numerous emotions can be evoked in a design when economy of material and space are not an issue. In meeting wih Greg Lynn's studio I was often greeted by a puzzled look when I asked the student "why" their design looked the way it did, as opposed to "how" they had mixed the features or geometries currently in fashion. Often, to ask "why" is not relevant in an architect's motives any more than it is for mountain climbers, except that instead of explaining "because it's there" the unsaid rationale is "it wasn't there before I made it."

This would no doubt sound familiar to American car designers of the 1950s who would have agreed with their extravagancies. Now the culture of car design and architecture seem to be switching focus, and at this rate the car designers will abandoned the perfect surface before their brethren in architecture have had a chance to be converted. Meanwhile young architects seem to be gaily enjoying their newfound freedom from the canons of their predecessors and are in no hurry to embrace new dogmas from the car guys.

On the other hand, there are some new examples of dynamic surface treatment that might be fertile ground for the future of both car design and architecture. With Berlin-based architect Frank Barkow, a graduate studio I co-taught at Harvard Graduate School of Design tasked the students to interpret the BMW GINA philosophy and technologies for a new type of suburban housing. Once again, we attempted to unite the car and the suburb into a single holistic (and aesthetic) phenomenon much like Frank Lloyd Wright had attempted in his origi-nal Broadacre City treatise. The students used the dynamic, flexible nature of the GINA skin to bring the social implications of material con-sumption and a lifestyle of changing spatial requirements into the public context—there is no hiding your excesses when your house grows fat containing them!

The results were exciting and very personal, much like the original GINA Light Concept Car. Moving Surfaces provide a new challenge to the domain of both the car designer and the architect: what are their standards and ethics if the influence of the customer *post facto* becomes the new *ipso facto?* Are we practicing good architecture or car design if the user dramatically manipulates and changes what we deliver? What happens when the param-eters for these shape-changes are known only to the house or car itself, and it acts on its own volition? Then the question of "why" things do what they do cannot be left unanswered.

Quo vadis, perfect surface? Perhaps there will be an end to perfect surface in the car design sense, no more relevant to the image a car projects than well executed buttonholes are to shoes today. Time and culture move on, and in a future of public-owned shared vehicles, any car design statements beyond, "Climb in, I have been Sanitized for your Protection," will be superfluous.

As a car designer, I would like to think a certain fascination with excellent craftsmanship and

80

sculptural elegance will always be in demand, and that the discipline of perfect surfaces will enjoy an unexpected rebirth. But for a Phoenix of perfect surface to rise it must first burn, and I truly believe that instead of lamenting inevitable change now is the time to turn up the fire, to make our creative experiments more inspiring, more audacious, more courageous. Car design and architecture should continue to work hard to excite each other, and perhaps in that way find a new common ground that inspires us all.

Character lines up, head lights closed on GINA Light Visionary Model

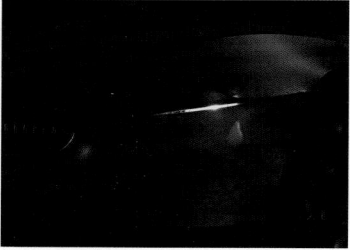

Character lines up, slightly opened head lights on GINA Light Visionary Model

Character lines up, slightly opened head lights on GINA Light Visionary Model

Character lines up, head lights opened on GINA Light Visionary Model

Chris Bangle (director design BMW group) explaining the GINA Light Visionary Model

Character lines up, head lights opened, widely opened engine cover on GINA Light Visionary Model

Character lines up, head lights opened, doors opened on GINA Light Visionary Model

Character lines up, head lights opened, doors opened on GINA Light Visionary Model

82

Tail lights, rocker panel and rear elements in normal position on GINA Light Visionary Model

GINA Light Visionary Model's interior with tilting instruments

Adriana Monk

Experiential
Design

In the design of cars and boats the basic challenge of harmonizing form and function is amplified. These high-speed sculptures demand an exterior identity that is recognizable in the blink of an eye while the interior must be timeless and pleasantly tactile. The interior must entice on first glance, but it is the test of living in the object that ultimately confirms whether the design is a success-inside and out. The experience of these types of objects must exceed all expectations.

When one embarks on such an experiential design journey, there is a certain sequence of steps to follow. I call it the "ThreeDee" (3D) process. In designing interiors in motion, the process can be broken down into three main steps. First, DIVE into the project and the brand. This is the research stage that contributes an understanding of the task at hand. Then DEFINE the goal by outlining the specific design philosophy and parameters. Finally, implement these elements to DESIGN the product. This results in a three dimensional expression of your analytical and creative work.

Having said this, as we know, creativity cannot be captured in a mathematical formula as a great deal of the design process is intuitive. Despite this, many corporations still search for a design recipe to guarantee the next icon. Market research to gain insight from the general public certainly does not alone yield good design. As Henry Ford summed it up right from the start: "If I'd asked my customers what they wanted, they'd have said a faster horse." Today, there are few companies who have found a way to produce good design innovations that the market is comfortable with. Apple is a good example of promoting design without compromise. Their products exude clarity. This is echoed throughout their packaging and their brand communication so that Apple's identity promotes a unified purpose.

DIVE

To implement the first step of ThreeDee, it is essential to dive into research of the specific project and the brand, determining the most prized values. These will set the tone for the experience of the product that is desired by the company and the user. The design of a yacht is a good challenge in this regard because part of its luxury aspect is the fulfillment of the

dreams of each individual client. Similarly, my design of the interior of a Rolls Royce, Jaguar, or Land Rover certainly adds up to more than simply wood and leather cladding. The design language is formed by the values of the brand and the desires and needs of the user.

DEFINE

"Lincoln low, Lincoln lean, Lincoln lovely." This was the tagline of Lincoln cars in the 1960s, three words that sum up the essence of the brand and can be translated into a set of design parameters. My mission in 2000 was to make the Lincoln brand appealing to a younger generation. How could we make the Town Car more than a New York limousine? The brand's heritage speaks both of innovation and of sophistication. Edsel Ford had an instinctive liking for dignity in a car, but dignity that reflected its purpose. In 1961 President Kennedy was driven in exquisite style in a four-door convertible Continental. Originally conceived as a Thunderbird (T-Bird), it was stretched and had a few additional doors, setting an enduring industry-wide design trend towards cleaner more functional styling. After winning

Adriana Monk "taping-up" Lincoln Navicross seat mock-up

numerous industrial design awards, the 1961 Lincoln was considered a piece of design excellence destined to be a classic. Wrapped in glamour with optimized restraint, it was one of the "Big Two" contenders in the luxury market, and its reputation was enhanced around the world. Even Pablo Picasso owned one.

The legacy of Lincoln's strong aesthetic heritage was the foundation for defining the new Lincoln design language. It was appropriate therefore to look at other American design classics. Consequently, the Charles and Ray Eames Lounge Chair was my choice: steambent wood, an innovative use of material; the clean form, a distinct style. Thus inspired, I designed an evolution of seats for the various Lincoln showcars as one of the building blocks for the second ThreeDee step of defining the design philosophy. The recognition of the strength of this new Lincoln design language was underscored by the fact that my seats for the Lincoln MK9 were independently displayed in 2000 at the Museum of Contemporary Art in Los Angeles, for the exhibition, "Retro-Futurism." They were shown adjacent to the Eames Lounge Chair, and needless to say, this

was a very proud moment of my design career. The new Lincoln design language I helped to establish epitomized driving in style in connection with cutting-edge technology. Even the dials were a synthesis of analog beauty and digital technology, representing the visual refinement of the individual polished chaplets and needles, coupled with the precision and clarity of a digital display.

The mission to design five Lincoln showcars in five years was to pay homage to the stylish early days of the Continental, yet bring the brand forward into the twenty-first century. Having thus defined the parameters, it was simply a matter of implementing the design directives in different models including a coupe, a four-door sedan, a PUV (Personal Utility Vehicle), an SUV (Sport Utility Vehicle) and a convertible with a retractable hard-top.

Culmination: DESIGN

Sir Henry Royce stated: "Take the best that exists and make it better. If it does not exist, design it." The values of the brand can be translated into design parameters, which in turn

Experiential Design

Photo of Lincoln MK9 Seat at the Museum of Contemporary Art in Los Angeles, for the exhibition, "Retro-Futurism" in 2000.

help establish the design language, reinforcing the identity of the brand. A good example of this is the clever disguise of an umbrella in the door of the 2003 Rolls Royce Phantom. This is just one of the quirky British design details that underscores the brand. These special touches are set off by the copious amounts of wood on the dashboard and doors, which overtly express opulence. Finally, the wrap-around settee in the rear compartment provides the comfort of your own private lounge. Living in London for a very intense year of "immersion" was the only way for me to define the future look of Rolls Royce under its new ownership in such a short time frame. When you work hard and play hard you get inspiring results.

Similarly, the design goal of the Jaguar C-XF was to realize and represent the brand's new design vision in a most abstract and creative way, yet still use very traditional materials like wood and leather. To create a black tone-on-tone interior that was somber and sophisticated I used charred poplar wood. The finished wooden panels were scorched to a perfect black hue that enhanced the grain beautifully and clear coated for protection. The black leather was embossed with a carbon fiber texture to display the technical prowess of Jaguar while maintaining the warm touch of leather. The logo on the dashboard epitomizes the essence of this project: it reduces all design motifs to a few strong and recognizable elements. Thus this pure flourish of just two brushstrokes captured the Leaper (the leaping jaguar) and became the new mascot. Because of its strong graphical impact, the logo was embellished with a few more curls to be re-imagined as a tattoo repeated throughout the car. It was etched into the headlamps and onto the tread plate, and even carved out of the rubber to create a unique tire tread. Like haute-couture, it was a showcar that expressed the brand's creativity.

Culminating with Design, the third step of the ThreeDee process is the most creative and the most rewarding because you get to express yourself by applying everything you have studied, absorbed and digested into an exquisite interior.

How can my ThreeDee guide be adapted to other design disciplines? In 2007 after ten years in the automotive world, I instinctively

applied this method as I shifted gears to design floating sculptures for the luxury company Wally. Their yachts always adorned my wall of inspirational images ever since Wally B and the 118 Wallypower first graced the waters. Today, I run my own business Monk-Design, using the ThreeDee formula to guide me through new projects. It boils down to doing your research and having a concept for everything you do.

SPACE

The quest to find and to define space in the design of moving vessels is a constant challenge. Space becomes an illusion; it can be reshaped to enhance the feeling of comfort using new technologies in lighting. At the same time that it appears to make an interior more spacious, light can offer a tranquil setting to ease the mind. My experience sculpting interiors with light came from finding ways to optimize space confined by automotive restrictions. For the Jaguar C-XF, I designed a cool black cocoon with intense attention to materials and details. To make it feel spacious, a glowing aquamarine headliner gives the impression of diving into the sea immersed in ethereal tranquility. These types of effects translate well to seafaring vessels. There are different ways of capturing light to brighten dark spaces. For example, glossy white interiors enhance light reflections. Also, if a small space is split into horizontal layers according to shape, color, and/or material, the width appears to increase. This enhanced linear elegance whether on a large or small scale, has a major effect on perception and therefore can alter emotional states. It has been the goal of each of my projects—whether automotive or nautical—to attain the desired emotional impact.

Yacht interiors offer the comfort of home combined with the lure of adventure. Many yacht owners enjoy the familiarity of a floating villa and thus furnish and decorate their boats to look like their homes. However, the special feeling of being on a boat is demonstrated through the strong connection with the sea and the water. These elements surround you and offer endless destinations. The sensations associated with being at sea can be heightened in the luxury interior. I always strive to enhance the view from within the vessel as much as possible while at the same time providing a safe haven

The Jaguar C-XF tread plate showing the evolution of the logo into a surface tattoo.

Interior of the Jaguar C-XF Concept car

Attention to detail on Lincoln Continental Concept instrument cluster.

Wally Sailing Yacht INDIO

Rendering of 100 ft racing yacht interior concept bow view

Conceptual sketch for 100' Wally

Rendering of 100ft racing yacht interior concept stern view

Rendering of 111 ft motor
yacht saloon fore view

Rendering of 111 ft motor
yacht saloon aft view

Rendering of 111 ft motor
yacht Master cabin

for those occasions when the sea becomes angry and tosses you around. The key is to strike the fine balance between design, comfort and safety.

With this in mind, I designed the interior of a privately commissioned 111ft motor yacht providing contemporary appeal without compromising on comfort. The structure and rigidity of the yacht is maintained by a repetition of cross-sectional ribs. In my design I am honest about the structure; instead of hiding it with cladding I expose the structure where appropriate. Throughout the 111ft motor yacht, I introduced a generous radius that blends the side walls to the ceiling. This enhances the visual height (since head room is always compromised on a boat) and when trimmed in black leather it has a picture frame effect where the view is the masterpiece and the frame "disappears." Small spaces require aesthetic tranquility, so I always keep my color palette to no more than three colors. When applied in linear continuity, the textures begin to play an important role.

Ideally there should be a seamless transition from the exterior to the interior. This is why the teak, which graces all exterior decks, flows through the saloon all the way into the master bedroom and then down to the master bathroom. A central strip of leather-hide flooring runs throughout the main deck, adding a luxurious feeling. It also weathers beautifully. Again, leather curls up behind the bed where the headboard transitions into the ceiling, creating a ribbon effect.

The master bathroom, situated in the bow of the boat, is an example of the optimization of a restricted space. I kept the walls and ceiling gloss white, and the carbon fiber benches become storage that disguises the cross sectional boat structure. The stone-textured wall gives a luxurious spa feeling with a Modern touch. It is in fact a thin ceramic tile, which again has minimal weight implications.

MATERIALS

The inherent properties of each material should be highlighted. Teak is the best wood for marine application as it is seeped in natural oils and, if well maintained, does not deteriorate with the harsh conditions of sun

Rendering of 111 ft motor yacht Master bathroom fore view

Rendering of 111 ft motor yacht Master bathroom aft view

91

water and salt. It also feels great on bare feet, providing traction but no splinters. On hot and sunny days it absorbs heat but never burns your feet and in rain and storms it becomes wet but never slimy or slippery. The combination of these amazing characteristics has not been replicated, as yet, by any manmade material. Although there are interesting ways of chemically inducing these properties into standard lumber, the demand on teak remains substantial in the yachting business.

Carbon-fiber is an equally fascinating material but for other reasons: its structural rigidity, its light weight, and its inherent beauty of black strands of carbon woven into an intricate mesh and captured in a clear resin. Since there are amazing "fake" carbon imitations, I like to expose this precious material when I use it to enhance the feeling of authenticity and to demonstrate its structural capabilities.

In addition to altering visual and spatial perception, details of form can be tactile. Cell phones and medical equipment, in particular, demand an appealing shape combined with a highly functional human interface. The concern for tactility is shared by automotive companies, which often find inspiration in consumer products that have a much shorter time to market. Consequently, the car, which can take up to 5 years of development, will never be as technically advanced as the cell phone, in terms of connectivity and interface. This became clear to me while doing product design at Designworks/USA, a BMW subsidiary. Not surprisingly, the automotive department with their top-secret designs stirred my creative instinct and I began to venture from products to cars. Thinking on such a large scale continues to bring new insights to me. In a car interior I am confronted with a large canvas that houses a myriad of products, where every single detail becomes an obsession. Every button and knob in the automobile is crafted to function individually yet must lend into a pleasingly cohesive interior. Details should not dominate the whole, but rather complement one another to craft a holistic interior space.

Furthermore, the overall concept should be evident in the smallest details. The haptic feedback of a rotary knob milled out of a solid chunk of aluminum as it clicks with a purposeful sense of precision is subliminal and sublime. The thin line of light that surrounds the buttons on the Jaguar XF center stack glows turquoise to illuminate its location for practical and safety reasons, exudes calm and expresses design harmony with the rest of the interior. Upon closer inspection, each detail should entice and thrill. The trend for understated interiors requires special attention to details in everything from stitching on fabric to the hue of light. Simplicity can only be found when all the options have been explored and complexity has been reduced to a few, strong, graphical elements. As Leonardo da Vinci said, "Simplicity is the ultimate sophistication."

Experiential Design is the culmination of the ThreeDee process—dive, define, design—to provide a perfect balance between knowledge, practical wisdom and intuition. A successful design creates a "love it...live it" experience.

Quang Truong
Jessica Varner
Brent Martin
Lasha Brown

Case Studies

Fluid Motion
Quang Truong

Fluid Motion uses the sleek curvatures and composite material logic of high end yacht design to bring fluidity to architectural form. The structure, which interlaces carbon fiber, glass, and aluminum is positioned so that the interaction between the landscape and the section is seamless. The shapes are inspired by hull construction technology as well as high performance high modulus textiles. These forms and strong materials are designed specifically for fluid motion: speed through water.

The building's skin takes its form from the textile industry and, at a fundamental level, from shark skin. Like shark skin, the cladding is composed of hundreds of similar, but distinct teeth. As they bend around the building's form each unit dramatically catches and reflects light. From any distance the active surface appears as a rippling, wet, glossy form.

The section is defined primarily by the large open volumes needed to house the equipment and processes of yacht fabrication. The main features of the large programmed volumes are suspended within the space. In this way the ground is the medium, much like a boat to water, so that the relationship between the ground and the structure is seamless and ambiguous. The program of the factory is situated both visually and functionally within this medium: materials are brought in from the urban edge, processed, composited, and reformed to slide effortlessly into the water.

96

Early sketch of site

Aerial view from above Gas Works Park

Rendered view as seen from the water. The curvatures of the roof surface take on the sky color, bending the reflection to just touch the ground plane.

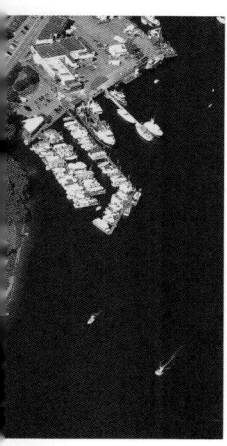

Rendered view of factory as seen from adjacent neighborhood. When the entire building is in view the roof reads as a smooth continuous surface, overwhelming the reading of the individual modules.

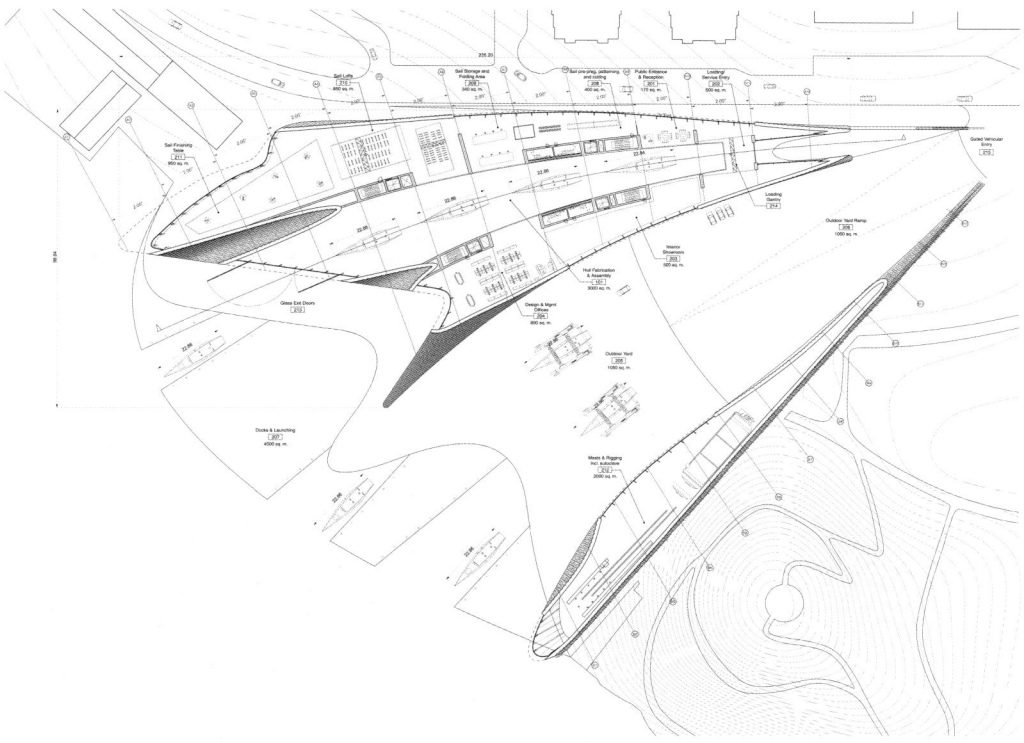

Architectural plan of factory floor

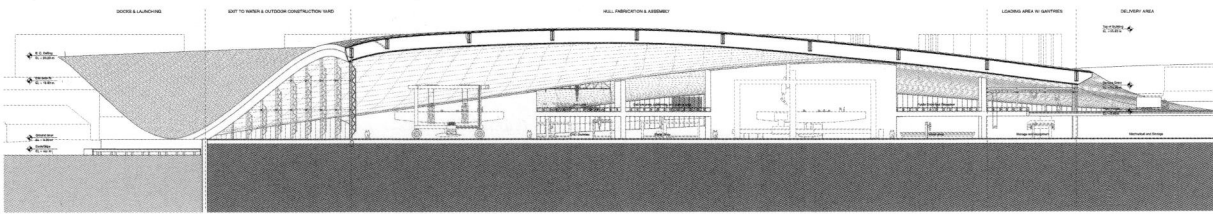

Architectural section along hull fabrication and assembly

Water Wall
Jessica Varner

Fluid dynamics software enables this acoustic panel design to achieve its aesthetic intentions and maintain extremely specific control of sound wave reverberation. Large undulations in the surface reflect larger sound waves and small holes absorb and refract smaller sound waves. The panel, developed in a seminar with Mark Foster Gage, is part of a carefully calculated acoustic system designed to control the sound qualities of a concert hall, which I designed in a studio with Frank Gehry. To ensure the success of both the performative and aesthetic goals of this panel, a number of different software platforms come into play. First, fluid dynamic studies that are analogous to the travel of sound waves were used. From this, similar to recent developments in stealth technology, the panel is able to react to a range of information by using highly precise, though apparently illogical, curvatures. This piece in particular reflects and amplifies the lower frequency waves, while absorbing, dispersing, and effectively dampening high frequency elements. Using similar logic, large-scale changes can be made to the overall acoustic envelope and adjusting the panel textures accordingly works towards achieving ideal sound performance.

The process of fabrication begins with a three-part mother mold milled with a five-axis robotic arm. A Corian sheet is then CNC milled with the hole pattern generated from the fluid dynamic tests. The mother mold is used to thermoform the Corian sheet to the exact profile. The result is a robust acoustic panel.

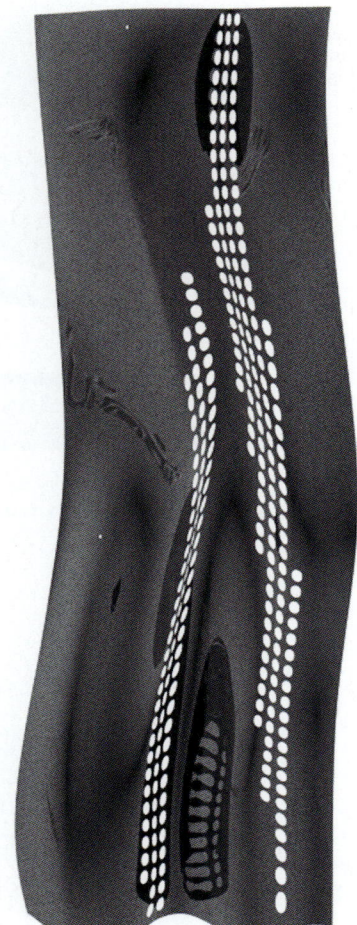

Digital rendering from the same 3D model used for digital fabrication

CNC mill cutting perforations directly from digital file

Five-Axis KUKA CNC robotic arm with end mill cutting positive MDF form to be used in thermo-forming of Corian panel

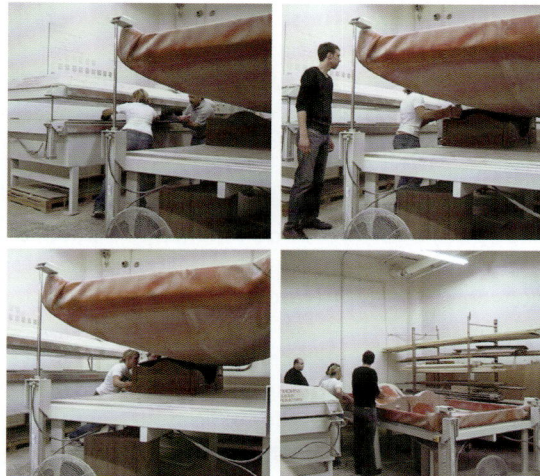

Thermoforming of custom perforated Corian panel on positive MDF mold

Close up of perforations in Corian panel

Speed Form
Brent Martin

Speed Form steals the tricks of a transportation designer: speed forms, black-tape elevation design, clay modeling, and digital fabrication. In transportation design a speed form is a physical model precisely crafted to study the visual impact of movement. They are dynamic directional forms whose carefully manicured surface bends reflections and elongates proportions to hasten the eye across the gleaming body. Black tape elevations are quickly generated gestural curves made of thin tape across a workable mylar surface. The technique allows the compositions to be developed, tested, unpeeled, and worked ad infinitum. Applied to architecture, these tools enliven the relationship between the designer and the building.

Traditionally in architecture, the whole is conceived to be greater than the sum of its parts. This design is intended to explore the ramifications of casting an entire building using the infinitely variable mold technology employed by manufacturers of high performance composite sails. Without joints, the building's visible relationship to the ground becomes malleable. The finite elements of traditional architecture including walls, floors, windows, openings, and columns become hard to define. There does not have to be a direct relationship between part and whole if there are no evident parts and only a whole.

The design offers a structural exterior surface that allows for light, air, and circulation. The roof dives down to make courtyards and otherwise define the space of the interior. A composite performative skin, with structure embedded as fine ribs within it, allows the structure to carry long spans and assist in the delivery of interior services. For example, the shell acts as a host for objects and even performs as a crane to move large objects around inside the factory. Speed Form not only borrows an understanding of surfaces from transportation designers, but also learns new techniques for incorporation of surface features and structure into an architectural composite.

Learning from the craft of transportation design, a model carved out of clay is a digitally integrated form test. The clay model is carved using the elevations as drivers in the design.

Several 3D scans of the model are made and aligned. Using the mesh from the 3D scanning process, a NURBS model (a polygonal model that has surfaces wrapped over it) is built to match for use in fabrication and rendering. Changes are made digitally, tested in clay, rescanned and repeated.

The building spans some 600 feet on each of its three faces, each addressing a distinct condition: city, waterfront, and park. As in automobile design, the surface of the building uses break lines to negotiate the shift from reflecting sky to reflecting ground. It wraps from face to face, using continuous curvature, with the beginning of a new dynamic line instigating the movement of each new gesture. Such automotive design techniques give the architect previously unconsidered ways of understanding surface and will allow us to bring new intelligence to yesterday's blob.

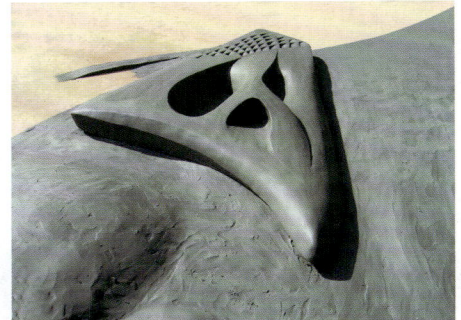

Clay model used to design surface—a technique used in transportation design. This model is 3D scanned to build the digital model from which all drawings and models are developed.

Aerial rendering of factory

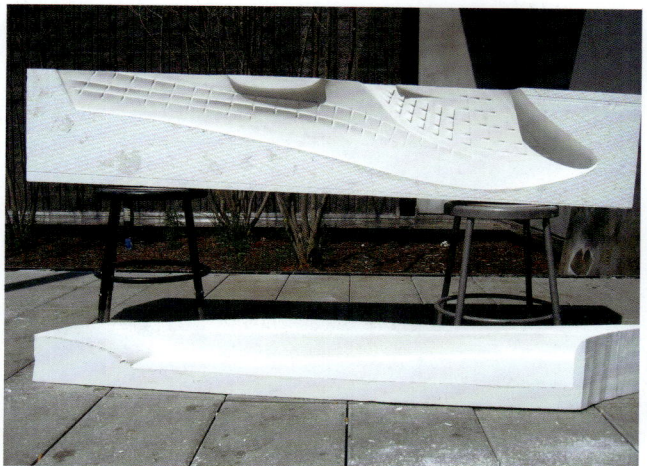

Two-part milled foam negative into which a positive shell is cast. This technique is similar to that used in rigid composite surface fabrication

Elevation of factory as seen from water. Learning from automobile design, the building has a carefully designed break-line—the horizon line in the reflection on the surface.

This sectional model uses carbon fiber to produce an extremely thin membrane with highly articulate apertures.

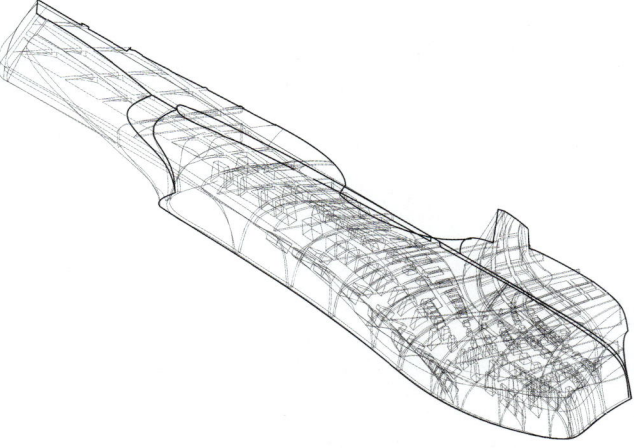

Isometric projection showing bulkhead configuration and skin perforations

Roof of factory showing skylight apertures and courtyards for outdoor fabrication yard and showroom

Twenty-First Century Shed
Lasha Brown

With the provocative program of yacht manufacturing and a site as loaded as the Gas Works Park in Seattle, Washington, Twenty-First Century Shed begs to be more than a functional enclosure for a factory. The floor reacts to the earthen mound of the park, continuing the topography to form an architectural plinth that extends out into the water. A large roof is laced with the functions of the factory, supporting the elements of the program and organizing the fabrication process. Ultimately, the building is a twenty-first century shed set atop a sculpted landscape.

This shed takes on the problem of surface as well as service. Unlike a typical shed, which stands as a large rigid volume, the skin of this mercurial span is articulated through folds and creases. As in automotive design, the surface organizes visual perception, encouraging the eyes to rest on longer break lines and hurry through tight curvatures with quick reflections. Functionally there are no pleats around the lower levels in order to meet the occasional need for privacy. All light enters through a series of skylights that are designed to catch the views. In turn, these apertures are sited specifically to enhance the image of the building from the surrounding bridges. The distant vantages display the building as a whole, further encouraging the reading of the full surface instead of a series of assembled facades.

Integration of landscaped surface with building structure

Close up view of long span trusses and roof substructure

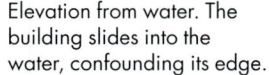

Elevation from water. The building slides into the water, confounding its edge.

Elevation from Gas Works Park. The low surface registers an almost water-like image in its position at the shoreline.

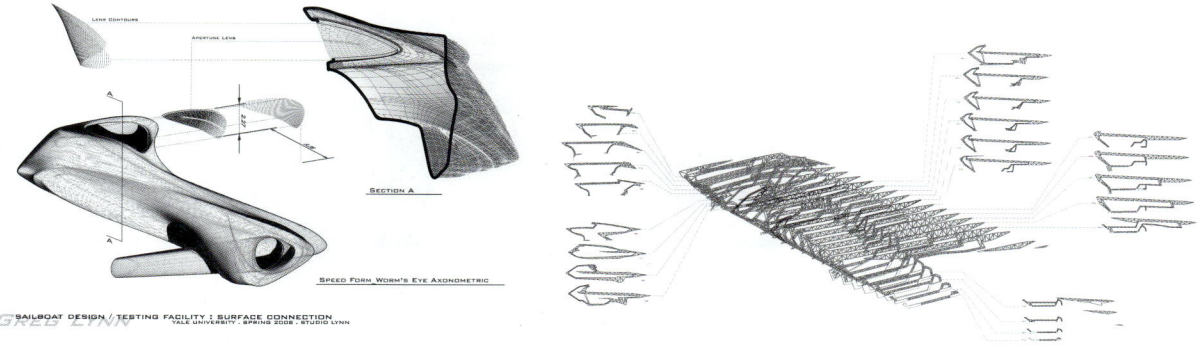

Surface aperture study

Diagram of structural truss system used for long span of factory floors

Factory floor with structural
bays supporting CNC
gantries for use with sail,
hull, and overall fabrication

Highly reflective
compound
curvatures
of building
envelope warp
the reflections of
the ground and
sky, creating
dynamic visual
movement.

Software

In architecture, the decades surrounding the millennium were about software for software's sake; fetishizing the forms that seemed to leap from the pages of a new digital catalogue. Polygonal meshes, digital surfaces, blobs, scripts, and versions, all scuffled to gain ground in architectural discourse. This period of experimentation has evolved into a new era focusing on infinitesimally precise and very real digital craft. Today's software gives designers the ability to talk to the machines that make things real. Previously we gawked at the abundance and freedom of form that was possible with this technology, but now designers are working with these tools in full scale. They are looking to these new digital tools for unprecedented precision from design to production.

Now with such high stakes, it is time to reassess the relationship between the designer and his tools. In the following section Mark Foster Gage argues that software, borrowed from a variety of design disciplines, is enabling the production of a new language of form. With a wealth of computational potential, it is the designers' charge to engage real aesthetic ambition and stave off the temptations of the prescriptive forms offered by highly specific software platforms. Design, he argues, must be more than an expression of the technology that makes it possible.

In a conversation with Greg Lynn, Frank Gehry discusses the ambient influences that take form in his designs. Gehry Industries, the computational workhorse behind the scenes of his architectural practice, was among the first to work fluidly between physical and digital models. By developing a link between the digital and the physical realms they set the stage for scaling computational precision to real construction practices. Inversely, it is the same technology that allows Mr. Gehry to develop a productive digital relationship with the sculptural forms that inspire him in the environment.

Lise Anne Couture, one of the principles and founders of the New York–based architecture firm Asymptote, writes on the importance of developing a feedback loop between design concepts and external factors. Consultants, physical models, digital analysis, and formal experiments are the pulse of the input used to tweak a design until it meets aesthetic and performative criteria.

It is only in recent years that software and rapid prototyping have enabled the designer to move so fluidly between the virtual and the physical. As design and fabrication feed each other, our digital dreams could quickly become real nightmares if not handled carefully and seriously. Design today requires learning a new formal language, honing these new tools and wielding them with great focus.

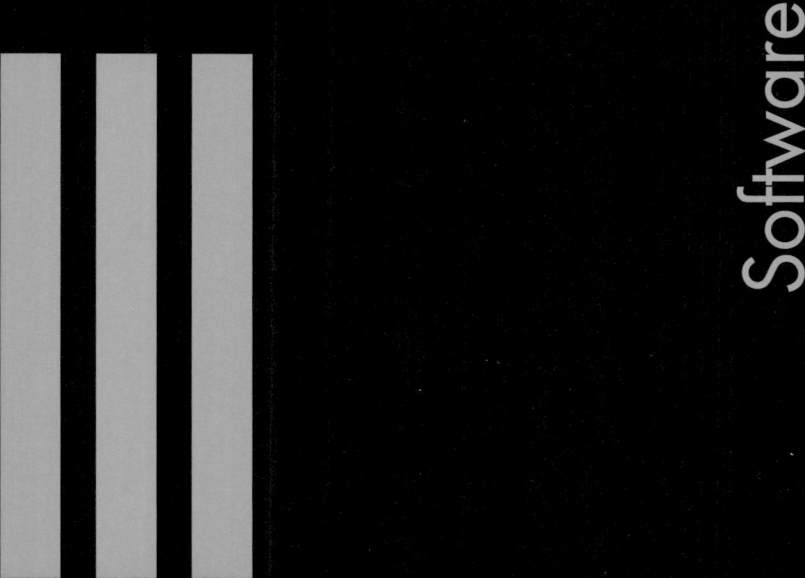

Software

Mark Foster Gage

Software
Monocultures

" It is a mistake to think you can
solve any major problems just
with potatoes."
—Douglas Adams

While originally Incan-cum-Peruvian in its ancestry, it was in Ireland that the potato suffered its greatest humiliation. Imported to Ireland in the late sixteenth century, the potato took firm root in the wet sticky soil that rejected most other significant food-providing forms of agriculture. By 1846 the *Solanum tuberosum,* known in Ireland as the "lumper" variety, had become as Michael Pollan tracks in detail in his 2002 book *The Botany of Desire* virtually the sole remaining variety of spud on the entire island.[1] While this monocultural strategy worked for nearly 250 years, offering easily farmed nourishment to a hungry and growing population, as well as independence from the domineering wheat of the British, in the end it was this same uniformity of genetics that caused the great potato famine that eventually claimed over a million lives and spurred a mass exodus of equally as many between the years of 1846 and 1852. Reliance on only one genetic strain of potato simply assured that a single virus could wipe out the entire crop species, which is precisely what unfolded in this six-year period.

Most systems of design, production, or analysis have a potato of sorts—the thing on which they rely a bit too heavily, that is questioned perhaps less than it should be, and that because of its sheer productivity, or its seeming innocuousness, exists just out of focus of prying critical eyes. Training at least our nose, if not a critical eye more focused on our own potential oversights, to the profession of architecture we might find that the potato for our contemporary hunger is our software—or more precisely, the standardized software packages on which we rely to do, well, everything. Software, like the electrons it pushes, occupies a multiple form of existence, being both and neither a physical thing as well as series of processes. This characteristic assures that, in a profession as generalized as architecture, software cannot be governed by any specific single group of people. Instead it draws on the talents of a vast range of programmers, debuggers, information technicians, and finally architects for its ultimate effectiveness. Because no single group can assume sole responsibility for its development, use, and therefore oversight in the architectural process, the position that software is maturing to play in contemporary architectural practice remains largely critically unchecked.

"Blazer Russet (A8893-1)" as determined by the Potato Variety Management Institute

Gage / Clemenceau Architects, SolarPod research project, rendering of solar pod, June 2010. Generated using a combination of automotive (Alias Studio), architectural (3d Studio Max), and special effects (Maya) software.

Addressing this lack of such critical oversight becomes increasingly important as the assimilation of digital technology, via software, dramatically continues to alter how the products of the architectural profession are designed, produced, documented, transmitted, approved, tested, and recorded. Despite this range of participants in the software-cum-building equation, ultimately it must be the architect who is responsible for the cultural impact and performance of final building, and accordingly for the biases of the tools and processes from which it was created. And without question, all aspects of the process that transpire under the architects supervision, from initial design to final fabrication have been affected by software. Through this process it is undoubtedly the production of standardized user-friendly architectural software, namely representational Computer Aided Design, or CAD programs, that have currently had the most dramatic impact on the day-to-day workings of the profession, and therefore, the built environment. Software packages intended to provide architects with easy access to the difficult processes of computation have been developed for everything from the aforementioned purely representational CAD systems to advanced parametric Building Information Modeling (BIM) systems that manage not only representation but material quantities, costs, supply chains, and assembly instructions, among other variables, in a single digital model. It must be recognized that although these programs are intended to manage information they have formal biases as well that impact the creative process. These biases arise because the software not only includes but also omits particular formal tools. No tool, software included, is free from leaving traces of its use. Accordingly, across scales and building types, the architectural design and documentation process for construction has been almost entirely rewritten in merely two decades. And, although BIM programs are gaining in popularity, the primary ingredient in this starchy standardized Vichyssoise has been the critically unexamined dominance of representational CAD programs.[2]

An obvious drawback of this particular digital revolution is architecture's dependence on an extremely limited set of software packages that give architects access primarily only to the Euclidean geometries on which the profession has traditionally relied. These CAD programs

operate by grouping together simple palettes of tools which allow designers to produce primitive shapes, in two dimensions and increasingly three dimensions, and alter, multiply, deform, and connect these geometries in the service of design. Circles are bisected to create arches, or further segmented into sections that are then recombined to produce more complex curves- albeit all still products of the original primitive. This poses the problem that the emerging built environment is being produced, almost exclusively, by the limited commands and limited geometries available in standardized architectural software packages.[3] The irony here is that while the computer has enabled vast advances in the formal opportunities for architectural design, never before have architects relied so heavily on standardized interfaces of design that obscure these new formal freedoms. This may be inadvertent, but it has certainly limited the design palette of the profession, and, as a result the aesthetic parameters of the built environment are being dictated largely by tools included or omitted by software engineers.[4]

Even with the best intentions, the most popular of these CAD programs, unavoidably, become fertile ground for monocultural development. They offer design and representational tools to architectural offices coupled efficiently with the formatting options to facilitate direct translation of this design language into the dialects of standardized contracting and fabrication. This is not a sinister proposition, as much as it is one governed by a primary interest in economic, contractual, and constructible efficiencies as opposed to ambitions of formal diversity in the service of performance or other forms of architectural innovation. So architecture finds itself today standing tall, and proud of its recent technical advances in its own vast and never changing field of genetically identical spuds. Responsibility here lies not with the software companies, who provide for the demands of the profession, but with the profession of architecture itself. The discipline has done little to challenge the increasingly constricting demands of economic efficiency that devalue architecture as merely a cost-per-square-foot container for program.

The Irish lumper was by contemporary standards a small, bulbous, and rather ugly looking tuber and is entirely unfit to carry the analogy of a contemporary architectural culture so perfectly geared to meet the expectations of efficient corporate material production and contracting processes. Expectations for standardized building practices in our current moment of the twenty-first century require simple geometries that allow for the use of a limited palette of regularly sized, easily purchasable, and readily deliverable products. From these standardized systems, shapes, and parts, architects attempt to arrange the *appearance* of a customized artistic vision or in more fashionable architectural parlance: a unique solution to a set of given programmatic or other performance-based problems.[5]

Therefore, our potato of today needs to be of the Russet Burbank variety, which is far larger, more uniform, and therefore more corporately efficient than the historic lumper. The Russet Burbank, to reverse the analogy, is the standard CAD package of potatoes, and as such lends itself more readily to being cut into predictably uniform and inexpensive shapes for us to consume—namely the nearly 28 pounds of French fries that each United States citizen consumes on a yearly basis.[6] The economics of America's love affair with french fries dictates a radical monoculture of tuber uniformity that covers nearly one million acres of land in the United States, a mere dollop compared to the 134 million acres of area currently covered with architecture in the United States. Simply stated, one of the largest land-covering products that humans produce, architecture, is now more than ever a vast monoculture of forms. Our dominant architectural software packages produce this through their very genetics. As the ultimate desire of standardized architectural construction, including factory made windows, suites catalogue issue doors, thirty-foot structural grids, and a whole host of design decisions that default to the properly formatted availability of standardized materials and construction processes, ensure vast formal uniformity across the American landscape.

Again this cannot be considered a problem of the software or building material industries as much as a shortcoming of an architectural culture that demands nothing greater from these immensely technical and productive industries. The introduction of BIM software to the playing field is often described as a significant improvement over the CAD programs of yesteryear. If

judged on production and economic efficiency, this is absolutely true, and BIM will likely replace CAD in the future. The problem of this progression is that although BIM software is significantly more complex than the CAD programs, it can manage but not produce as equally complex and innovative forms. That is to say that CAD and BIM programs represent two generations of information management for the profession of architecture, but they are not designed to capitalize on the computer's ability to perform as a design tool. As such, their palettes of tools, and reliance on primitive geometries and simplistic repetitive commands are oriented towards information management and constructability rather than design ends. As the complex interconnections between data and form become more intricate, the sacrifice at the moment is that the shapes and options for producing them are even further simplified. If not by the software, then this is being carried out by its users who are now confronted with significantly more variables that require input, and taking shortcuts on inputting these variables, through simplistic icons for instance, results in the sacrifice of the potential original qualities of the form itself. Of late, the profession seems only too eager to make this sacrifice in order to streamline design and production in the service of efficiency, time, and profit. Architecture now more than ever needs to be defined as the addition of value, cultural or economic, to building and not to be seen as the enabler of its lowest common denominator economic production.

Early resistance to this trend was asserted by a small contingent of architects in the early to mid 1990s, including Greg Lynn of Greg Lynn FORM, Hani Rashid and Lise Anne Couture of Asymptote Architecture, and Jesse Reiser and Nanako Umemoto of Reiser + Umemoto. These architects employed new forms of experimental digital practice to develop strategies to counter the emerging monoculturalism of standardized CAD forms and their associated geometries.[7] This ignited the struggle for the role the computer would occupy within the profession: would it be merely a drawing tool to better organize representations of geometries that are already familiar to us? Would it be a tool to analyze performance criteria in the service of efficiency? Or would it be used to introduce new families of geometry and form in the service of innovation? The original artillery used to bolster an architecture of innovation was the adoption of software from other industries of design typically unconnected to architecture. Early experiments at the turn of the millennium involved software programs including Alias, Softimage, and later Maya, Rhino, and Mudbox to introduce new formal vocabularies into the discipline of architecture. They provided new palettes of tools that not only were based on the simple geometries dominant in architectural CAD platforms, but that also imported the polygonal and topological tools responsible for character animation in Hollywood movies and similar extra-architectural sources. These more mathematically robust tools were joined by later experiments with software programs that allowed access to other new languages including the precise surfacing tools used in automotive design (AliasStudio), the polygonal faceting languages of origami folding programs (Pepakura), and the mechanism to hold subdivision surfaces together found in later releases of Maya.

On one hand, the adoption of software programs from other industries offers a way to overcome the limitations, or at least geometric

biases, of architectural design software packages. On the other hand, because these programs come from outside the discipline they lack tools for architectural scale, their techniques for translation into physical form are undeveloped, and the formatting systems are not adequate to manage the vast numbers of components and component types needed for architectural projects. Therefore, the strength of these programs—that they are non-architectural in origin—is also, predictably, their Achilles heel when they are faced with the task of producing work for construction and fabrication. Furthermore, when inexperienced practitioners rely on such programs to produce architectural form, they run the risk of producing non-architectural forms that overtly evidence the original intent of the tools. In inexpert hands, building proposals can adopt the unarticulated continuous faces of animated characters, and architectural givens, like openings for windows become difficult to resolve in sympathy with these new surface languages. A tangential drawback to the use of these tools is the unintended associations with biological forms. Tools designed to produce digital creatures and animals for blockbuster

Gage / Clemenceau Architects, Estonian Academy of the Arts, rendered elevation, March 2008. Designed using Alias Studio— a software program specifically designed to manipulate "Class A" automotive surfaces.

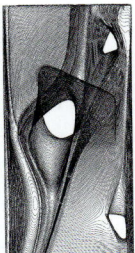 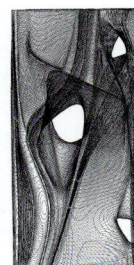 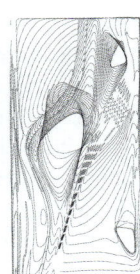 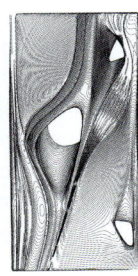 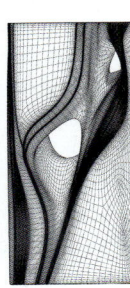

Gage / Clemenceau Architects, Estonian Academy of the Arts, topological analysis image, March 2008. Analysis of curvature complexity for prototype panel fabrication.

movies frequently produce biological-looking constructions for architecture–even when producing such forms was never the intent of an architectural project based on overcoming known limitations of form, whether architectural or animal. This pulls the work into existing discourses of animality, biology, and natural metaphor that are unlikely candidates with which to understand *new* languages of form. And so tools designed to produce automotive surfaces produce architectural projects that look like cars, and tools designed to produce paper origami sculptures began to produce architectural projects that look like paper origami sculptures. These are not fruitless pursuits, only indicators that each of these newly adopted programs is, in fact, a monoculture in its own right that possesses limited tools designed for limited functions. An image of unfolding paper that can be created in the software program Pepakura is perfect for paper which has imperceptible thickness, but it does not translate well into a discipline such as architecture which requires, even revels in through poche, the substantial thickness of its surfaces.

While some of the most provocative developments in recent architecture have come from translating the techniques and tools of one discipline into another via software, following such a model without limits offers what amounts to only a slightly larger variety of software monocultures from which architects can choose. As architects working in this vein wrestle with the translation of the software, they will find in their pursuit of more control that much is to be discovered in the problems that arise. This discovery, however, should be done with a critical understanding of what is at stake and should not be considered (as is currently the fashion in many architectural form-finding exercises today) mere architectural "play." Also, it is hoped that as software companies like Autodesk acquire other design programs such as Maya, Mudbox, and Alias Studio, they will continue to fold the tools of these programs into existing architectural platforms, to create a more formally robust software that maintains architectural applicability.

A parallel computational trend within the profession has emerged in recent years: custom digital scripts are being authored by architects themselves. Albeit difficult and unwieldy to

learn, early versions of such customizable software interfaces were present in packages like Maya Embedded Language (MEL) and more recently in RhinoScript. As architectural scripting continues to grow and migrate out of imported software into new intelligences of its own, it introduces a wealth of new formal avenues for architecture, increasing dramatically the ability for the profession to manage complex aggregations of multiple forms— whether varied or graduated and intricately interconnected. From languages of swarms and piles to webs, Voronoi foams, and booleaned bricks, scripting has become the definitive language of variegated multiples assembled into larger architectural wholes. Theoretically this development has been charged with giving architecture access not only to parts but also to a finer grain of small particulates—the stuff from which stuff is made.[8] This stuff however exists within its own world of rules since scripting is, by definition, a myopic process that isolates a problem so that it can be overcome with a limited set of precise and interrelated algorithms. Such myopia risks becoming a new hermetically sealed environment, where outside influence is weak if not non-existent.

So scripting does not translate into a comprehensive language that facilitates the emergence of architecture, although that is certainly the hope and sometimes the claim. The diversity of components that contribute to an architectural project in the fullest sense demands not only changes in formal and scalar degree, as scripting in its current form provides in spades, but also changes in component and material type, with which these processes currently have more difficulty. That is to say that the component arraying and modifying strategies employed in the acts of scripting produce variations that are sometimes vast in scale and shape, but these scaled and reshaped components are always grandchildren of an original geometric primitive, or data set of points, and are beholden to the limitations inherent in that original form or network, as well as to the script's ability to translate data accordingly.

The techniques of scripting offer architects the ability to write their own formal grammars and associated rules, but in doing so, architects forgo the infiltration of foreign expertise into the protected fickle codes of digital conduct which govern these scripting efforts. If the use of software from other disciplines bears the Achilles heel of formal languages with intelligences other than those of architecture, then the drawback of the scripted product is that it exists with no expert intelligence from any design discipline other than that inherent in the original code or parametric data set. The *ex nihilo* act of scripting conducted by an individual architect as opposed to a suite of professional computer programmers also runs the risk of being an amateur endeavor. Although worthwhile, architects as scripters are generally the product of architectural schools rather than computer programming departments and are accordingly inexpert at the acts to which they are dedicated, particularly when compared to actual experts in those disciplines. Because these tools are so new to architecture, amateur knowledge in a field of no existing knowledge is perceived as expert, even though this may not be the case. A more promising model is one of collaboration between experts in architecture and programming—each versed in the nuances of their respective professions—to produce architectural form that exhibits expert intelligence from both disciplines.

Gage / Clemenceau Architects, Kaohsiung Pop Center, graduated rain-screen detail, July 2010. Skin produces variations in color and geometry based on complexities of curvature—calculated in a custom designed RhinoScript.

113

Gage / Clemenceau Architects, Kaohsiung Pop Center, aerial rendering, July 2010. Generated using a combination of automotive (Alias Studio), architectural (3d Studio Max), and special effects (Maya) software.

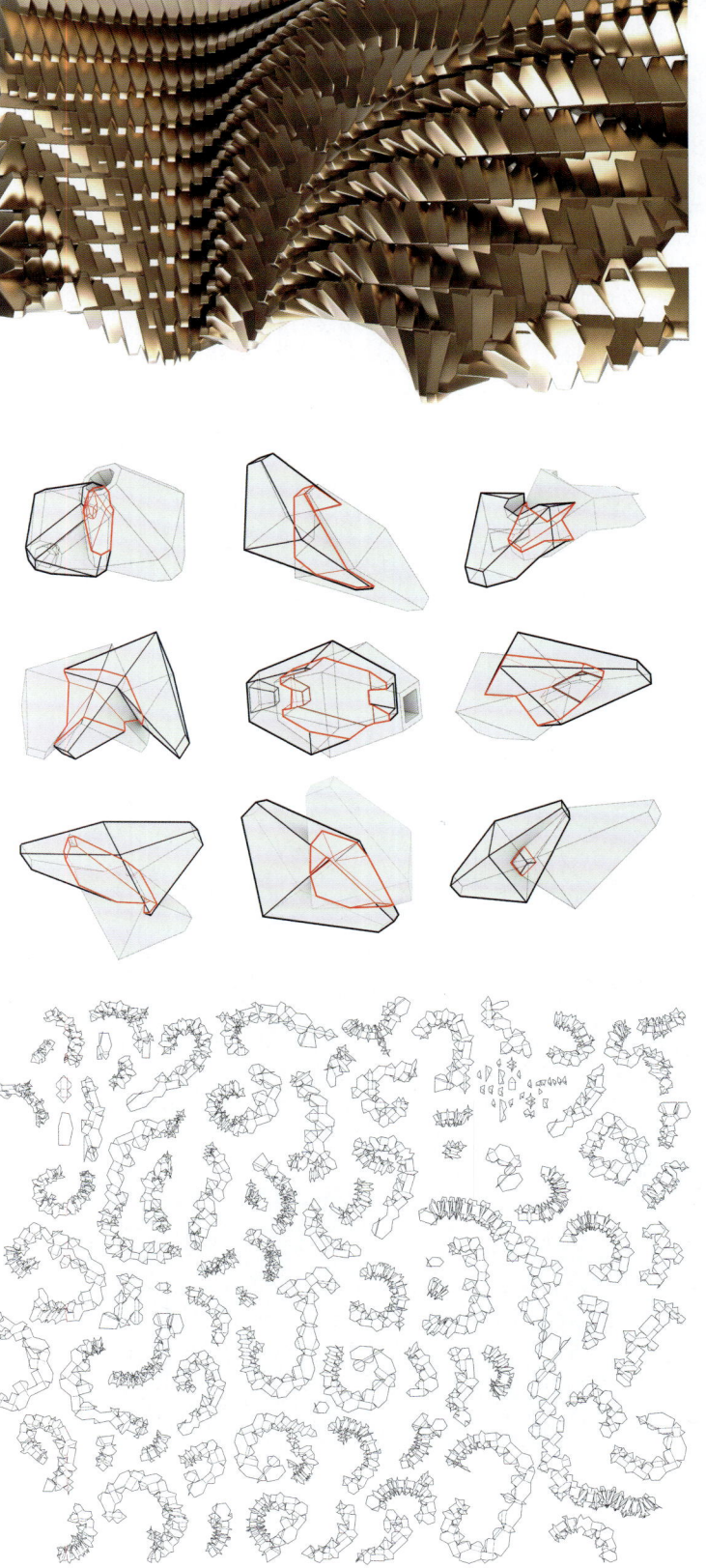

Gage / Clemenceau Architects, Parawall Research Project: an investigation of Parametric Aggregation Strategies for Complex Architectural Surfaces, perspective rendering, 2009. Individual bricks are repositioned parametrically to respond to various gravity and force loads generated in a retaining wall scenario. Research conducted using Rhinoscript and Maya MEL, Maya Embedded Language.

Gage / Clemenceau Architects, Parawall Research Project: an investigation of Parametric Aggregation Strategies for Complex Architectural Surfaces, joint analysis, 2009. Individual bricks are booleaned from neighboring bricks to produce geometries conducive to stacking. Research conducted using Rhinoscript and Maya MEL, Maya Embedded Language.

Gage / Clemenceau Architects, Parawall Research Project: an investigation of Parametric Aggregation Strategies for Complex Architectural Surfaces, unfolded brick fabrication drawing, 2009. Individual bricks are unfolded in the Origami software program, Pepakura, to be lasercut and assembled from flat materials.

A fusion of these strategies to avoid becoming a monoculture is emerging between software importing and scripting that offers some hope in assuaging the deficiencies of both. Recently some programs have introduced simplified scripting platforms that encourage designers and programmers to customize the performance abilities of the programs themselves. Simplified graphic interfaces like Rhino's new scripting interface, Grasshopper, make modifications and scripting tools more accessible to architects who are unfamiliar with the language of writing custom scripts. However, there are drawbacks to this approach as well. The introduction of simplified palettes and organizational relationships reduces the potential for open-source customization of the program. So another monoculture, albeit one of icons and pull down menus that help build scripts instead of icons that perform transformational functions, is born. This makes such a program better suited for educational use as an introduction to relationships between form and code. Certainly a full collaboration between disciplines would result in more fruitful outcomes.

Many of the aforementioned systems include parametric intelligence, currently architecture's most *au courant* topic. The early scripting program, Bentley's Generative Components, as well as a parametric scripting program currently in development by Autodesk are efforts to build software programs that are more directly dedicated to the instant visual manipulation of form via custom scripts. Parametric intelligence provides for architectural form to be derived and altered using interconnected data sets, as opposed to transformation of the form by the architect. With parametrics the modification or addition of data, when linked with form, has the capability to alter or produce forms without requiring any willful input from the architect. This is touted as a positive development for architects who define architecture as the solution to cleverly identified problems.[9] In a perfect yet very rare parametric world, a data set can lead to the production of an "ideal" form that best suits the performance criteria required by the data. Following from this, if a collection of forms is produced that best suits the performance criteria required and then one form is modified, the other forms in the set will update accordingly in order to best match the new configuration to the criteria of the altered

data. This method requires architectural form to be the product of posing and solving problems through data set relationships. The form is limited by the parameters set in the equation, and like writing script it is inherently isolated within one discipline, as it is only through the problem itself that expertise can be derived. Therefore, all architectural intelligence that can be expected from the result must be written into the problem as it is first established. The other noticeable difficulty with the strategy of parametric intelligence is that the intelligence must have an initial primitive shape or similar network of point locations on which to operate because form rarely emerges *ex nihilo*—even one derived from the demanding expectations of massive amounts of architects' accumulated data. As such, parametric design strategies rely on the development of primitives that in turn are modified by the associated data and therefore are limited to the languages of primitives available within the software, like CAD, or architectural intelligences of the given data sets themselves.

Importers, Scripters, and Parametricists. It is of course a mistake to even initially separate these efforts into such carefully segregated groups, as the groups and tools are actually more intertwined than such partitioning suggests. Nonetheless, all certainly fall under the rubric of architectural design systems emerging from "the digital." It is slightly ironic that each group seeks primarily to overcome the standardized digital tools that currently dominate the formal output of the profession. Even more ironic is that in doing so according to the myopic limitations of their own solutions, each, further isolate their methodologies from the discourse of architecture at large, which needs to be more encompassing than any of these solutions can alone suggest.

The first decade of this new century of architectural design is off to a good start, and our options are increasing, as is our expertise. While these options, taken as a suite are currently much more of a monoculture than a rainforest of diversity, the possibilities offered by all three trajectories are aiming in the right direction. At the moment, however, it is clear that the inclusion of these strategies into the profession increases the variety of types of practice possible but rarely diversifies the practices themselves. In fact, the nature of architectural propriety has produced a contemporary discourse carried out in segregated monocultural books and equally monocultural symposia, where scripters meet with scripters, importers meet with importers, and parametricists with parametricists. At its most extreme, each group is publishing edited books of allies' work, and congratulating itself on its particular brand of digital toolmanship, even asserting that it is the future of the profession while the other strategies clearly are not.

It is important to consider not only how these developments fit into contemporary architectural practice but also to position them in relation to the architectural discipline in its fullest historical and cultural sense. The Renaissance concept of the architect/artist as solitary genius, originally created to separate these artistic castes from that of the more common craftsmen with which they had been previously associated, is mostly to blame for this manner in which architects have mistaken the role software might play in the profession.[10] Architecture in the Post-Alberti Renaissance was a culture of individuals. It is even more so today as both architects and the public recognize vast formal vocabularies by the names of singular practitioners. One has only to describe a building as Meisian or in the vein of Peter Eisenman, Zaha Hadid, or Rem Koolhaas to call to mind an entire corpus of projects and buildings which hundreds, even thousands of people, were involved in producing. That is to say that architects are historically invested in producing a recognizable monoculture in their body of work, which we more artistically refer to as an architectural "signature." Signatures, in this architectural sense, govern the selection and management of particular geometries, materials, colors, design tropes, and historical references.

A tragedy of the digital project, all strains considered, is that signatures are no longer determined by these historical architectural variables and instead, are now being largely governed by software selections and individual technical discoveries. A particular imported software tool or even the simplest Rhino script can produce results that are mistaken as architectural signatures because of their initial formal novelty. Software importers may remain loyal to particular software packages and even particular icons within those packages.

Scripters can squeeze an entire family of projects, small and large, from the most common digital codes that are as frequently found in online clearinghouses as they are self-authored. At the moment there is an entire generation of architects who choose to be defined by a narrow range of software monocultures. These monocultures already are producing a predictable sameness in formal, programmatic, and sustainable projects alike. So inculcated are we in the practice of individual signatures that architects now curate identity through these discovered, and closely guarded, software tools. The tools of computation promise to offer architecture the greatest infusion of formal possibility ever seen by the profession. Yet the model of appropriating monocultural software processes for the purpose of developing clear monocultural signatures assures an ironically vast uniformity should the current methods of architectural software use be maintained.

In the emerging twenty-first century, after several decades of rehearsing old scenarios of architectural practice with our new digital tools, architecture needs to now adopt new modes of practice that capitalize on the complexity and contemporaneity of these tools. In doing so, it assures that the formal and organizing gifts of the computer are not distilled into a series of selfishly protected monocultures, or ubiquitously accessible icons, but instead are allowed to flourish throughout the profession in the service of greater diversity and opportunity that reflects an architectural culture of actual ideas. Architects need to resist the proprietary mentality of software and begin to use these tools not as ideas in and of themselves but in the service of more encompassing architectural agendas. Such a mentality will necessarily need to contradict the master narrative of individual signatures in favor of a more expert and cross-disciplinary collaborative approach to the profession. Instead of the identity of an architectural office being determined by the original digital skills of its founders, architectural offices should forgo software allegiances in favor of an exploratory ethic to use software to address the newer, more complex, and more important questions which architecture should be authoring and addressing in the emerging territories of the twenty-first century. Our problems and concerns are not the same as those of the various Modernisms of the early twentieth century on whose geometries, processes, and expectations of efficiency we still largely dwell. Our software tools and the geometries and processes with which we design should not merely be more efficient ways of organizing and building the forms of yesteryear. Instead they should empower a new generation of conceptual thought, theoretical speculation, sustainable responsibility, and formal production. Architectural offices must develop a culture that uses digital expertise in the service of great ideas and does not rely on the software by virtue of its novel production to function as a proxy for such ideas, particularly when the underlying biases of such software remain unexamined. Only then will architecture bring more options to bear on the larger ambitions of our new millennium than a handful of mere potatoes.

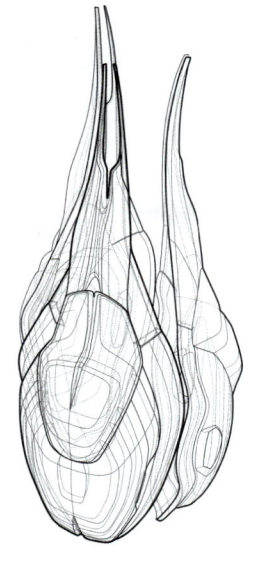

Gage / Clemenceau Architects, SolarPod research project, x-ray drawing illustrating panel seams calculated based on material size constraints. June 2010. Generated using a combination special effects (Maya) software rendering combined with Autocad 3D compositing.

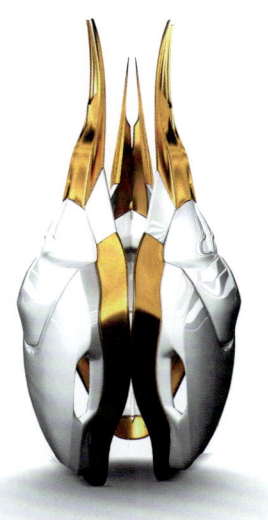

Gage / Clemenceau Architects, SolarPod research project, closed pod elevations, June 2010. Generated using a combination of automotive (Alias Studio), architectural (3d Studio Max), and special effects (Maya) software.

Gage / Clemenceau Architects, SolarPod research project, open pod perspective, June 2010. Generated using a combination of automotive (Alias Studio), architectural (3d Studio Max), and special effects (Maya) software.

1

For an insightful history of the potato see Michael Pollan, *The Botany of Desire: a Plant's Eye View of the World* (New York: Random House, 2001), 183–238.

2

William Mitchell in his essay "Thinking in BIM" outlines the development of BIM software and correctly notes that preceding CAD packages had begun to evolve by "shifting their emphasis from the construction and editing of two-dimensional drawings to the construction an maintenance of complete and consistent three-dimensional models, by replacing rigid geometry with object-based parametric modeling, by providing increasingly sophisticated facilities for associating non-geometric properties with geometric entities, by integrating engineering analysis software and by supporting sharing and transfer of information among various members of design and constructions teams." As CAD programs developed these abilities, however, their efficacy was still largely based on Euclidean geometries. While parametrically interconnected to data sets and possible to be visualized in three dimensions, the icon and primitive based systems for drawing geometry in CAD remained formally simple. See William Mitchell, "Thinking in BIM," *A+U: Architecture and Urbanism* (August 2009), 10–13.

3

Certainly any tool, including CAD comes with its own bias towards production, but never before in the history of architecture has the same tool been so uniformly used to govern such a significant majority of the process from conceptual design through design documentation and furthermore be accepted almost without question by the profession at large. William Mitchell refers to some historic examples of earlier tools and their biases in his "Thinking in BIM" essay. See page 11 specifically.

4

That is not to say that computation via CAD did not increase the formal diversity of the profession, only that it fails to capitalize on the exploitation of the computer's ability to provide dramatically new formal languages. CAD largely kept previous geometric mentalities and coupled them only with new systems of drawing and management that did capitalize on the strengths of computation.

5

Although I have my own doubts on architecture's reliance on mapping problems as a primary vehicle for the production of form, see Gage, Mark Foster. "In Defense of Design," *Log*, no.16 (Spring/ Summer 2009), 39–45.

6

Statistics are taken from "French Fry Consumption in USA on the Decline for First Time" in *Quick Frozen Foods International* (July 1, 2002).

7

It should be noted that while Frank Gehry's office was also pivotal in the introduction of computation into the profession, the manner in which they transfer handmade physical models into the computer is more allied with the use of the computer as a management tool as opposed to a design tool, which was ultimately the goal of these practitioners.

8

For further reading that links processes to form via scripting intelligence see Sanford Kwinter's afterward essay entitled "Seven" in Benjamin Aranda and Chris Lasch, *Tooling* (New York: Princeton Architectural Press, 2006), 92–93.

9

See note five.

10

For the definitive source on the Renaissance reading of artists and architects as a separate class of artistic and melancholic genius see Wittkower, Margot and Rudolf Wittkower. *Born under Saturn, The Character and Conduct of Artists: a Documented History from Antiquity to the French Revolution* (New York: New York Review, 2007).

development of the panelization. We satisfied design intentions while fluidly updating and keeping an eye on the detailed construction logic of each panel, the communication requirements of the fabrication between design and fabrication, and both micro and macro cost metrics. In the end, when we bid the curtain wall, the bids came in at the exact same cost as a flat curtain wall because there was no mystery to the design. It was well documented and the contractors and consultants had been a part of the design process. Moreover, the building is nearly finished and there have only been around 250 requests for information (RFI's) for the whole job. Comparable towers of one million square feet usually have around 1500 RFI's. Each RFI usually means an extra cost for the owner. We did this with a lot of hard work, a superior team and a very powerful tool. I think neo-minimalism is like post-modernism and is a cop out.

Beekman Tower by Gehry Partners, LLP during construction

Greg Lynn   It is also so sad the way architecture used to have a lot of power even with sculptors, and sculptors who in the 1960s were interested in architects. Donald Judd and Richard

125

Beekman Tower by Gehry Partners, LLP during construction

Serra looked at architecture for inspiration to get out of the gallery space and then the next generation of architects decided to take inspiration from sculptors fifty years later and build it out of rare bogwood, to add value to it by sheer expense and the luxuriousness of materials rather than with spatial or formal quality. I really think it is reprehensible to promote that kind of opulent minimalism as being ascetic and contemplative at the same time innovations in form and expression are being attacked as being frivolous. For me, those minimalist details and extravagance of materials is frivolous because it is so cynical. But I have always hated minimalism even when it was "povera."

Frank Gehry   I loved it when I was younger, because when Judd and Carl Andre and those guys were doing it, they were making minimal sculpture that somehow made sense as a cleansing response to the post-war blitz. But to see it regurgitated now does not make sense. Now, if Judd was around, he would be championing it, I know. [laughs] And I do not know what Carl Andre thinks now.

Greg Lynn   Originally, that art came out of confrontations with established modern discourses, but the contemporary architectural minimalism is completely different as it is ameliorative. I love the visual and technical language that the computer introduces to design. I love what it has done to everything besides architecture. For example, the design of cars and planes has benefitted tremendously from the computer. The fact that I can talk to automobile designers, boat designers, plane designers, industrial designers, film makers, and video game designers all because we use a common digital platform and perhaps even a similar medium is really exciting. In particular, I enjoy the dialogue with design fields that are more connected with popular culture than architecture.

Frank Gehry   Well many people disagree with that optimism. Maybe because we are

friends and we sail I can see where you are coming from, but in my experience you are one of the only guys who takes the computer seriously and is trying to figure out an authentic place to go with it. How do we make architecture into something that will resonate and solve global problems like housing, and energy saving and the larger issues that we all have to worry about, which is the real stuff? Your approach is very promising to me.

Greg Lynn   Well, it is a funny generation gap, too. You understand it and care about it, but I think I am the oldest guy who actually models with a computer.

Frank Gehry   Really? What is everybody else doing?

Greg Lynn   Handing it off to somebody else to do. I think even the people who say they care about computers do not really know how to use one. They have their office do it. And I know you do not use a computer, but you have an innate understanding of what it can do from controlling the construction process to contributing to the artistic process, and that's incredibly rare.

Frank Gehry   Yes, but the old adage, "garbage in, garbage out" still pertains. You must really know what you want to achieve. What the world probably does not know is that you can make curvilinear shapes with a selection of materials, and the fabrication process is plugged in, you can make those things very, very competitive with archaic building techniques that we have been using for centuries. The breakthrough occurs once you have realized that there are no limits to the kind of shaping you can do; it is like being a kid in a candy store. That is what interests me and that is what I explore, but I am caught in the middle ground compared to where you guys are. My attitude now, maybe it's because of Abu Dhabi, is to go primitive. I have come totally around the other way. I am using big chunks of wood, big stone walls or raising pre-cast concrete walls. I do not use the computer to drive the design; we use it as a collaborative tool for the consultants and during construction. I assume that it will be used here in the same way that we are using it on our project in Paris for the

Architectural model of the
Guggenheim Abu Dhabi
by Gehry Partners, LLP

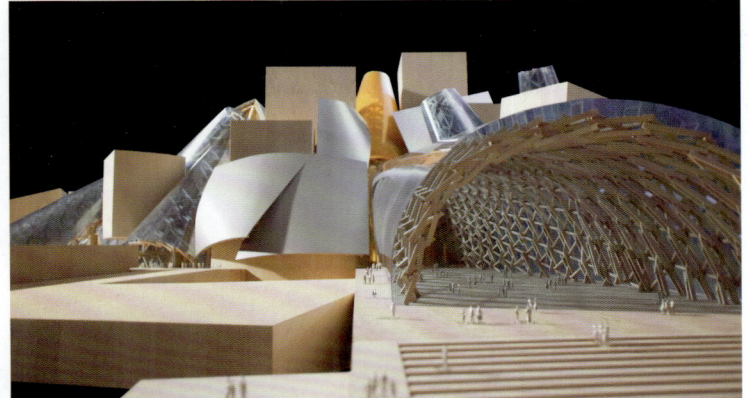

Architectural model of the Guggenheim Abu Dhabi by Gehry Partners, LLP

Architectural model of the
Guggenheim Abu Dhabi by Gehry
Partners, LLP

Architectural model of the Guggenheim Abu Dhabi by Gehry Partners, LLP

Fondation Louis Vuitton. There we have over 150 people using one model simultaneously to aid in the construction of the project, and the client has instant access to all sorts of metrics about the project. It is incredibly efficient.

Greg Lynn   It is beautiful that it is so intricate.

Frank Gehry   Yes. But it is still all very primitive. They are primitive models, let's say, though I don't know what that means. Maybe it's my age. I think I am looking for a kind of humanity in it that somehow gets lost when I see people making all of these shapes randomly and building them. Some of it looks like someone just snapped a picture on the freeway and built it. [laughs] We are working for Swire in Hong Kong, and we have an apartment building under construction for them. It is on the Peak on a beautiful site. I think it's going well. Gehry Technologies is working with Swire on other projects. For example for One Island East we saved twelve percent of the construction costs by managing the interface between the trades and the consultant and by completely eliminating change orders.

Greg Lynn   Gehry Technologies had a big impact on Hani Rashid and Lise Anne Couture's Yas Hotel in Abu Dhabi, and also on Zaha Hadid's building in Zaragosa, Spain. Technology is already making things possible that would not have been previously.

Frank Gehry   That is what most excites me. So far I have not made any money on it; I actually put money in it. Because, in fact I will be happy if it changes the game of technology in relation to globalization. I don't know if everybody realizes how globalized the art world is. Artists in Lebanon, Syria, Israel, Africa, and China all talk to each other. It is a phenomenon that we have not seen before in the art world—it has come upon us all of a sudden like a big surprise. And it is bigger than anybody realizes.

I just raised that with the Obama people. I said, "You know, here you are trying to figure out how to talk to Iran, and the artists are talking to each other already. There is a model of how to do it if you guys want to—the arts are a big deal for globalization. I went to Cape Town to

give a talk with the Fortune/Time/CNN Global Forum, but I was the only architect.

128

Architectural model of the Swire Hotel in Beijing by Gehry Partners, LLP

Architectural model of the Swire Hotel in Beijing by Gehry Partners, LLP

Lise Anne Couture

Feedback

Today a laboratory-like atmosphere can be found in many architectural studios where new territories are being explored and the types of architectural projects that are being pursued are expanding. With an enviable array of tools that are available for experimentation physical output now includes digitally produced models, component, and material studies to full-scale mock-ups. Collaboration with specialists and the integration of data back into the design process is allowing new and ever more intelligent iterations. The process of constant refinement and updating serves to achieve optimized performance and integration of all aspects of design including aesthetic, economic, structural and environmental. The process of architectural design continues to evolve as disciplinary boundaries are pushed to reveal informative overlaps with other design disciplines.

In addition to translating research and experimentation processes, moving between scales is another important strategy for uncovering new perspectives. At Asymptote taking on smaller projects is one way to test ideas that we may later translate to the scale of building. This is a particularly useful research strategy for us because the software and technology used for these studies is similar to that which we might employ at a larger building scale. We use the opportunities provided by installation and exhibition design, or object and furniture design as platforms for experimentation. These projects are understood as expedient forms of research that can inspire innovative approaches to the generation of form, surfaces, and effects. The smaller scale of these experiments also enables speculation and testing of new possibilities with respect to materials, fabrication techniques, and assembly methods, which include the potential of software to contribute to, and impact possible outcomes.

Digital tools are critical to the seamless integration of the design process and fabrication methods to enable the testing of designs and techniques, both with digital simulation and physical mock-ups. For example, the same software that we are using to test and visualize formal ideas can fluidly export information for the control of fabrication tools such as tool paths for laser cutters and milling machines. Digital blueprints are infinitely precise and editable. A design can be partially fabricated, or fabricated at a smaller scale to examine

visual and performative effects. This facilitates an iterative process incorporating the results and knowledge gained from one version to subsequent versions with the feedback loop potentially also extending from one project to another.

At Asymptote we take a keen interest in the techniques and strategies of other design disciplines as a means of generating new content that is unfamiliar to architecture. Applying the techniques of aeronautic, automotive, marine, and industrial design to specific project constraints such as physical and cultural context, program requirements, and the limitations (or possibilities) of building technologies can be the initial basis for architectural exploration. The variety of tools at the disposal of the architect along with a continually expanding range of materials, techniques, and strategies enable architectural ambition to push beyond the constraints of conventional constructability and communication of information to arrive at innovative and "optimized" tectonic solutions that are also aesthetically and formally provocative.

Likewise, the input of various professionals from specialty areas related to architecture is an indispensible resource for innovation and contribution to the design feedback loop of the iterative process. Incorporating cutting-edge technology and materials through the contributions of experts in areas such as structural, environmental, and facade design enables the architect to fully engage the possibilities that today's digital tools allow. Collaboration among architects and specialists who are each innovators in their disciplines enables collective resistance to conventional solutions and predictable results in all areas—from cost and constructability to form and aesthetics.

The cross-disciplinary influence of integrating digital tools into the process of architectural design has been an especially important driver of Asymptote's work. In early speculative works such as the I-Scapes, industrial design products that were conceived and developed with tools that are now commonly used by architects were interrogated and recombined as speculative architectural entities. Inspired by these design objects, the digital manipulation of surfaces and primitive forms resulted in architectural proposals made possible only by these digital

Lise Anne Couture

Software

modes of representation and modeling. Not only did the unfamiliar, yet compelling, tectonics that resulted make it clear that conventional and familiar methods of fabrication are no longer be adequate, but also that performance-based criteria could be integrated seamlessly into the design and production processes. Examples of this in industrial design include a plastic molded razor or high tech running shoe in which performance based criteria from ergonomics to material characteristics (fit, support, weight, flexibility, strength, tactility, breathability, density etc.) are completely integrated with the aesthetics and branding of the final product. Asymptote's design approach is informed by the integration of the performative with the cultural and physical that is evident in the industrial design process.

The Knoll A3 furniture system (2002) that overhauled the ubiquitous office cubicle was inspired in part by the I-Scape investigations, and the design and fabrication of the A3 system in turn influenced the design and construction of the Hydrapier Pavilion in Haarlemmermeer, The Netherlands (2001–2). This project that is inspired by the technologies

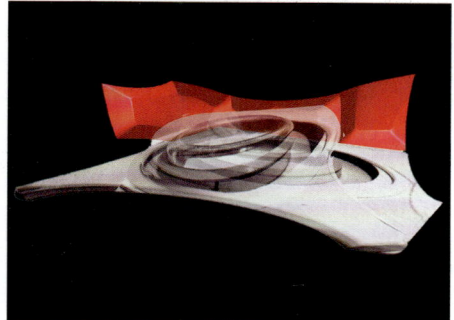

Iscape conceptual design model

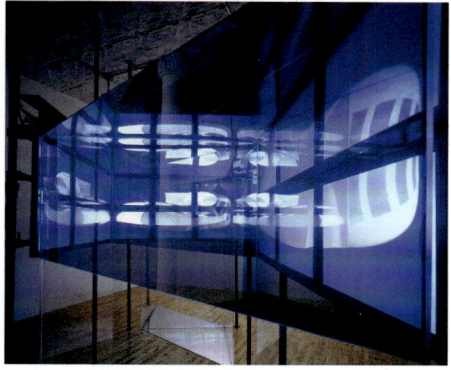

Iscape installation

133

The Knoll A3 furniture system

Exterior view of the Hydrapier Pavilion in Haarlemmermeer, The Netherlands

Below the transluscent ceiling of the Hydrapier Pavilion

of flight and hydra-engineering was initiated with an interest in the possibilities that digital tools offered with respect to form generation and looked to other relevant disciplines for material options and fabrication strategies. This early interest in performance-based design and parametrics led to further investigations in the field of aeronautical design, in particular, to derive strategies for the curved panelized cladding and structural support for its wing-like form.

At the building scale, the architect must also rely on the input of consultants to build intelligence into their design. The architect in effect becomes but one of several collaborators conducting research and development, however the architect is ultimately also responsible for coordinating and collecting input from all of the various disciplines, synthesizing the analytical data, recording results, and in the end recalibrating the architectural formula. Consultants draw on their expertise to bring new data to the table that refine, and in the end reshape, the potential outcome according to specialized criteria. By assessing such input as detailing, material selection, sustainability concerns, constructability, or building performance, the architect must determine the design priorities and parameters. In sum, the architect must design the process in order to design the building.

In Asymptote's Strata Tower project in Abu Dhabi (2006–ongoing), the twisting and tapering form of the tower was the primary strategy against which the different options for structure, cladding, and environmental design were tested. In the end, the synthesis of all these optimized solutions, drawn from each specialized area, provided the most fertile ground for innovation. For example the repetitive pattern of louvers of the exoskeleton was proposed as a strategy to mitigate the impact of the climatic conditions on a glass tower with 360 degrees of exposure. With the input of Atelier Ten as environmental consultants, the dimension and density of the louvers on the facade could be parametrically determined and subsequently varied depending on the orientation and required degree of solar control. The incorporation of such data and the optimization of the system impacts not only environmental systems but other aspects of the architecture as well. The louver pattern with its varied density

Rendering of the Strata Tower project in Abu Dhabi

134

also created a new asymmetrical composition on the facade, varying the architectural expression of an otherwise symmetrical form. Likewise the optimization of the structure and the rationalization of the glass panels of the building enclosure also offer new opportunities for spatial and architectural resolution.

While the outcome of the design process is certainly affected by the input and synthesis of various types of expertise, the methods used in the representation, translation, and ultimately, the physical realization of design concepts also have a significant impact on the end product. At Asymptote, architectural interventions at the scale of the interior have been used to conduct one to one scale research into this. The interiors of two of Asymptote's retail projects are the result of the use of certain software and the methods for transitioning from conception to documentation and ultimately to fabrication.

With the design of the Carlos Miele flagship store in Paris (2003), the 3D modeling of the curvilinear forms were constantly tested against the method of fabrication. In this case, borrowing from the ship building industry, a

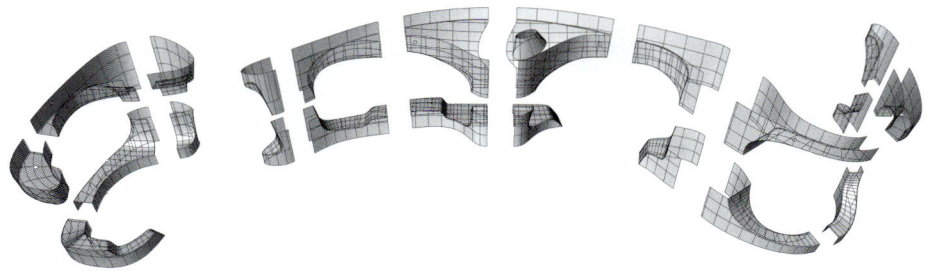

Drawing generated from a 3D model explaining the components of the feature wall in the Carlos Miele New York store

The Carlos Miele Flagship Store in New York's Meat-packing District

135

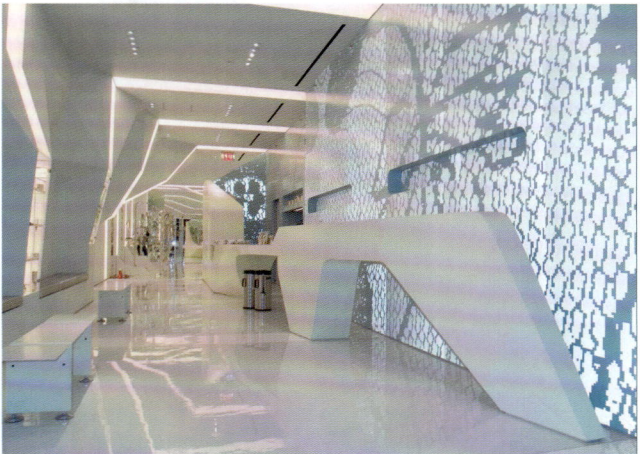

The Alessi flagship store in New York

structure was built from a series of ribs and fins that were laser cut using digital files extracted from cross-sections of the design models. This armature was sheathed by rigid composite panels that were finished to appear seamless. The process necessitated that the geometry be constrained to developable surfaces and secondly that these could be translated into a panelized skin system. The bending limitations of the sheathing material were being tested constantly, measured, and fed back into the design process to further refine the geometry.

In the Alessi flagship store in New York (2006), two types of geometric articulation were deployed to comprise a faceted interior shell that housed three-dimensional curved millwork. Both entailed the translation of three-dimensional data to facilitate the fabrication of the respective components. The walls and ceiling were modeled both digitally and physically to refine the desired effect of discontinuous sections aligned and connected to suggest an overall form under transformation. The digital models of the faceted surfaces were then unfolded and dissected to provide one-to-one scale templates to cut the sheet

material and build out the framing while the three dimensional data of the millwork models was translated directly to cutting paths for CNC milling machines. The choice of software that facilitates certain types of modeling or transition from design to fabrication, undoubtedly affect the outcome and require an understanding of the constraints inherent in the process and the materials to reach the full potential of the tools at hand.

Beyond experimentation to achieve certain geometrical and physical outcomes, smaller-scale projects and installations also serve to study and implement various spatial phenomena and material effects. The experimental work of the first I-Scape installation in 1998, along with other installations such as Off-sideOn (1999) and iScape 3.0 at Documenta X (2002), and more recently the Flux installation at the 2008 Venice Biennale, capture some of the interests that we have continued to investigate over the past fifteen years including the interplay of objects and the environment and the fleeting quality of one's apprehension of specific spatial relationships. These installations also investigate the relationship between

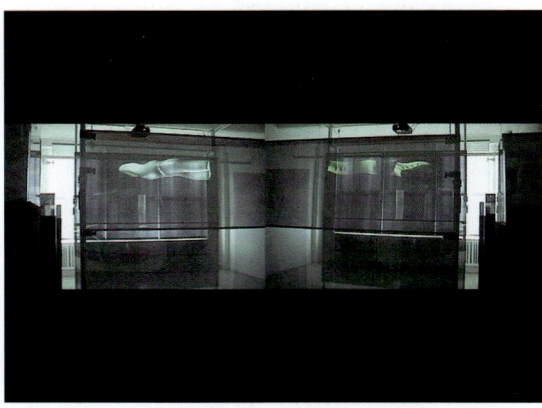

OffsideOn installation at the Henry Urbach Gallery in New York

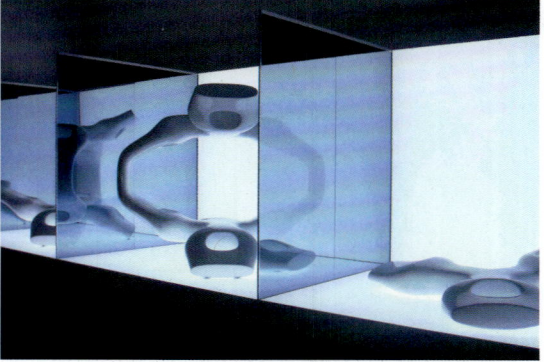

3 houses for the subconscious. Installation for the 2008 Venice Biennale

136

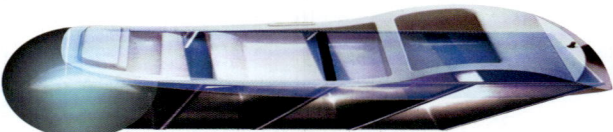

Documenta XI

Flux 3.0 M.Scape City Installation, 2002

digital material and the nature of form making, while the quality of the space of the installation itself is a deliberately confounding virtual/real environment.

In the exhibition design for a permanent interactive exhibition space for Volkswagen, information on Volkswagen's global finances and investments were displayed completely in the digital medium. We designed the presentation of the content, the digital interfaces, and the physical space in which the digital information is experienced so that the line between the virtual and the real became an interesting subject for exploration. The design concept played on this by building a physical version of a virtual effect: the reflection of built elements around a horizontal datum that traverses the entire space. As initially revealed in the digital models and subsequently in the built space, the exhibition space became a kind of strange wonderland, a virtual space rendered physical.

The notion of digital space and augmented reality is something that we continue to find as intriguing as the material aspects of our work. The concept behind the design of the facade at 166 Perry Street (2006–10) included celebration of the varied and vital urbanism particular to the West Village and New York City at large. The residential units are encapsulated within an elegantly sculptured facade of cascading glass and highly polished metal. The changes in light and atmosphere captured in the building's angled surfaces create an architecture that is in a constant state of animation. The facade's treatment allows for the dematerialized quality of reflections and the modulating qualities of light to prevail, forming an ever-changing exterior. On the surface of faceted panels the reflections of the surrounding urban context are constantly oscillating while the ephemeral qualities of changing light and sky are momentarily recorded. These effects and others, while anticipated in digital simulations and physical models, proved to be even more compelling in the one-to-one scale mock-ups and the completed construction of the building. As the unforeseeable can often be a positive aspect of the design process or outcome this too needs to be "anticipated."

With the Yas Hotel in Abu Dhabi (2007–9), the models and mock-ups proved indispensable not only in the aesthetics of the design but on

Variation in the refelcted image of 166 Perry Street, New York, 2009

166 Perry Street, New York, 2009

Approaching the Yas hotel in Abu Dhabi, 2009

multiple levels including structure, environmental performance, constructability, logistics, and lighting. The Yas Hotel's gridshell, which gains its strength from a double curvature is made of over 5,000 glass panels with a frame comprised of 20,000 steel components. A collaborative team of professionals, all specialists in parametric design within their individual areas of expertise including architecture, structures, and facade design, used various forms of modeling to rationalize and optimize the gridshell architecture. Strategies were developed to ensure that the design could be built without the need for a lot of costly customization. All components were dimensionally within the standards of mass-production, the number of different panel sizes was reduced to an acceptable level, and the design of a universal joint and a limited family of steel connections greatly reduced the number of required component types. Ultimately, these aided in streamlining fabrication and assembly. Furthermore, strategies were developed through an iterative process that satisfied technical and logistical constraints and were also used to develop and enhance the formal aspects of the design. In particular,

a parametrically-determined tolerance range for the gap between glass panels and steel frames greatly reduced the variation in panel shapes and sizes, and the parametrically determined angles of the glass provided optimum air flow for cooling and allowed for the integration of a sophisticated computerized light emitting diode (LED) array. Most importantly the optimization achieved aesthetic goals and created the desired profile for the gridshell's shimmering scale like surface.

An architect can never truly begin the process of design with a blank slate, whether intended or not, the reverberations of past experiences will be captured somehow in future iterations or projects. With the tools and techniques at the disposal of the architect, and the myriad of opportunities that can be used for experimentation and advancing research, various forms of output can be, and should be, continually mined for inspiration and usefulness in the broadest sense.

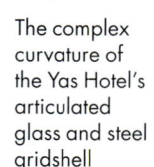

The complex curvature of the Yas Hotel's articulated glass and steel gridshell

The gridshell gains strength from it's complex curvature

Chiewhong Tan
Cody Davis & Patrick Lun
Stephen Nielson
Jon Cielo

Case Studies

Faceted Surface
Chiewhong Tan

Faceted Surface is an investigation of folded surfaces. Facets provide structural rigidity, spatial definition, and surface effect. A string of triangulated geometry crumples along a path and completely disintegrates upon reaching the center of the building. Throughout the building, seams in the geometry provide shaded apertures to reflect light deep into the vast space. Smaller triangles span the production halls and cradle the shipyard. Ultimately, it is the geometry itself that generates the innovative rigid structure and shimmering elevation.

Critical to the design process is a back-and-forth between physical and digital modeling. Maya animation software allows for an active modeling process so that shifting and tweaking the spaces would not slow the overall workflow. This flexibility enables a single three-dimensional computer model to be manipulated and tested with visualization software to achieve the desired effect. A simple piece of origami software brings this process into the physical world. The software uses the digital model to unfold the faceted design and instantly generate tool-paths for laser cutting, as well as assembly instructions. These physical models were an excellent method of testing the longspan challenges created by the program and the complex geometry.

A simple principle is proliferated in such a way that predetermining the outcome seems unfathomable. A marriage of digital management and physical experimentation allows a precision that evokes both calculated rationality and delicate intricacy.

142

Interior view showing long span showroom space at center of building and smaller definition at the shoreline

Interior view showing light penetration

Pleats in the surface create apertures to allow light deep into the space and add structural rigidity where necessary.

The dimension of the folds decreases as the spaces take on more human scale program.

Elevation of factory from water

Interior at opening to shoreline

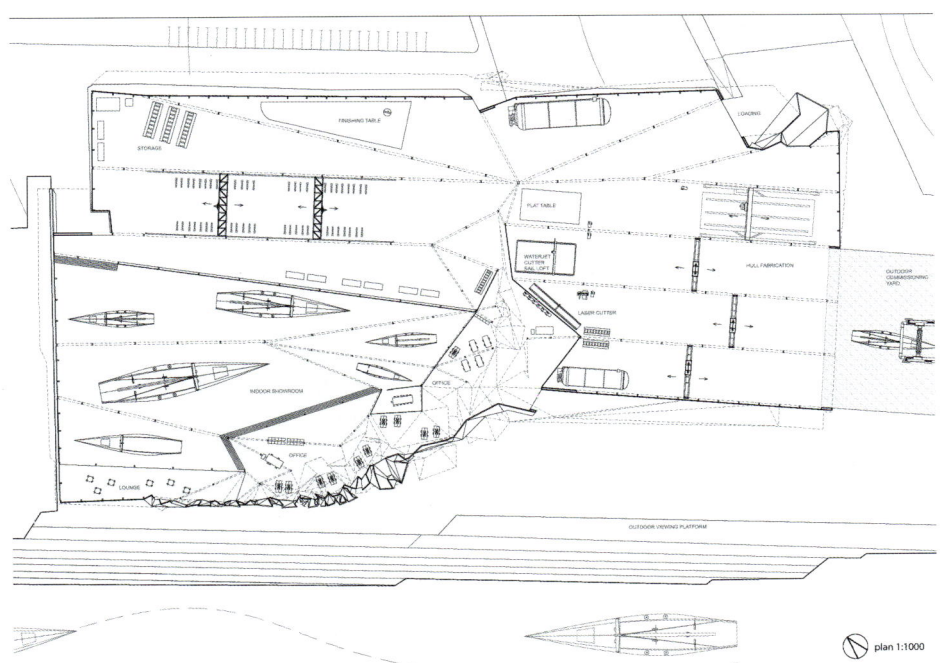

Plan organization follows the large structural roof pleats for fabrication program and smaller apertures for human program.

plan 1:1000

Charybdis
Cody Davis & Patrick Lun

Charybdis was an installation designed, fabricated, and mounted in Paul Rudolph Hall at Yale University. The challenge, which took the form of an independent study with Mark Foster Gage, was twofold: to develop a set of techniques for surface modeling in Maya that satisfies our outlined aesthetic criteria and to explore the capabilities and limitations of the five-axis KUKA robotic arm at the Yale School of Architecture. Such industrial robotic technology offers certain advantages for optimizing the fabrication process as well as broadening the range of curvature that can be achieved in modeled surfaces. Also, milling was not limited to a single vertical projection, therefore we could produce forms that billow, curl, and fold in any spatial dimension and could form and cut in 360 degrees around the shape's circumference.

Using Edmund Burke's *Philosophical Enquiry into our Ideas of the Sublime and the Beautiful,* we categorized and translated aesthetic qualities found in a range of contemporary design fields into formal nuances that would help us calibrate the techniques we developed. Through iterative testing of the robot we were able to establish parameters that would feed back into the subdivision model. The final form, a seven-foot tall spiraling vortex, attempts to exploit all of the motion capabilities of the robot along a single continuous line of variable thickness. At one end, slumped onto the floor, the mass of material is articulated with undulations that smooth into a single fluid strand. This comparatively thin segment is marked with creases that emphasize its spin into the air. Although the entire form was milled from a subdivided polygonal mesh, this portion had a single lofted non-uniform rational basis spline (NURBS) surface embedded inside of it. The motion of the robot was then associated with this piece of interior geometry. The mill would be positioned orthogonally to this surface while cutting the polygonal mesh to the outside. The vortex terminates with two openings that continuously connect two sides of the surface, with each portion milled by projection cuts from two sides, choreographed into one single motion.

Photo of finished piece

144

Five-Axis CNC robotic arm with end mill articulates to the surface normal to mill smooth, accurate curvatures

Still from animation used to articulate form

Finished piece seen from above

Finished piece showing dynamic expression

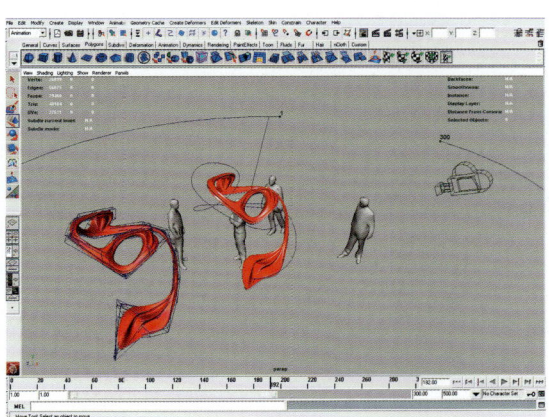

Screen shot from Maya animation and model

Finished piece showing scale as relevant to the body

Ornamental Mediation
Stephen Nielson

Ornamental Mediation is an exploration of the architectural problem of the building meeting the ground, or more generally of the horizontal meeting the vertical. In the Modernist catalogue this moment has often been disarticulated as absence or reveal, dissolving the joint into abstraction. The Classical, Baroque, and Late Gothic strategies of dealing with the intersection of planes are to articulate and emphasize the seam. Crown molding, capitals, bases, and rustication are all means of mediating between the two surfaces. In this project that mediating element, the ornament, will serve as an organizational, formal, and functional framework for the building. Thus it will escape being relegated to subservience to the primary vertical and horizontal surfaces. This particular trajectory can be understood as relevant to the high-end yacht industry through a discussion of mass customization, made possible through cutting-edge robotics and software agility. The future of production calls for refiguring values. Because fineness and craft will no longer have a one to one correlation with expense, and thus prestige and distinction, we might look to aesthetic value, even "beauty" as a means of evaluating design.

Ornament was abandoned in the Modern movement in part as a result of the stigma associated with the opulence of embellishment and its relation to the labor economy. The digital, through robotics and high-powered computing, enables the architect to bring ornament back to the table without a reliance on excessive labor or material waste. Opening this discourse offers architecture a rich vocabulary—one the common man, un-baptized in the lore of Modernism, can understand and appreciate. The efficiency of workflow overlap and robotic technology enables the production of ornament at minimal cost. In this instance basic panel fabrication is outsourced using data from a 3D file. Visualization software further smoothes the workflow by engaging client input. Raw building panels may be three dimensionally scanned to ensure consistency between the preproduction and post-effect digital files. Because of the infinite precision of digital data, the designer may continue to work on the desired effects late into the process. Ultimately, this method of information transfer alters the paradigm of typical construction documents. Detailed ornament that was abandoned by a certain ethic in Modernist architecture is made possible again through technological means, bringing beauty back to the discipline.

View of entrance from neighborhood approach

View from water

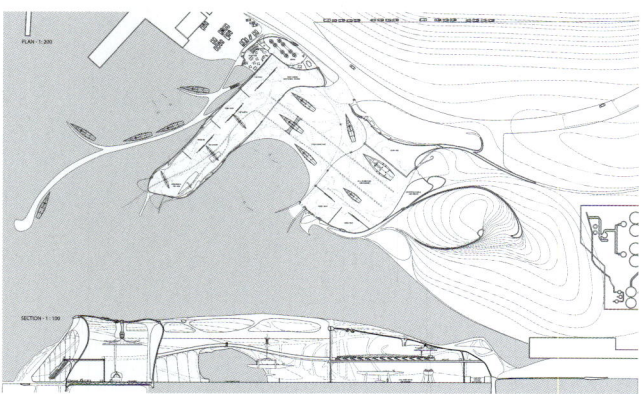

Ornament functions as mediator of landscape and architectural surface.

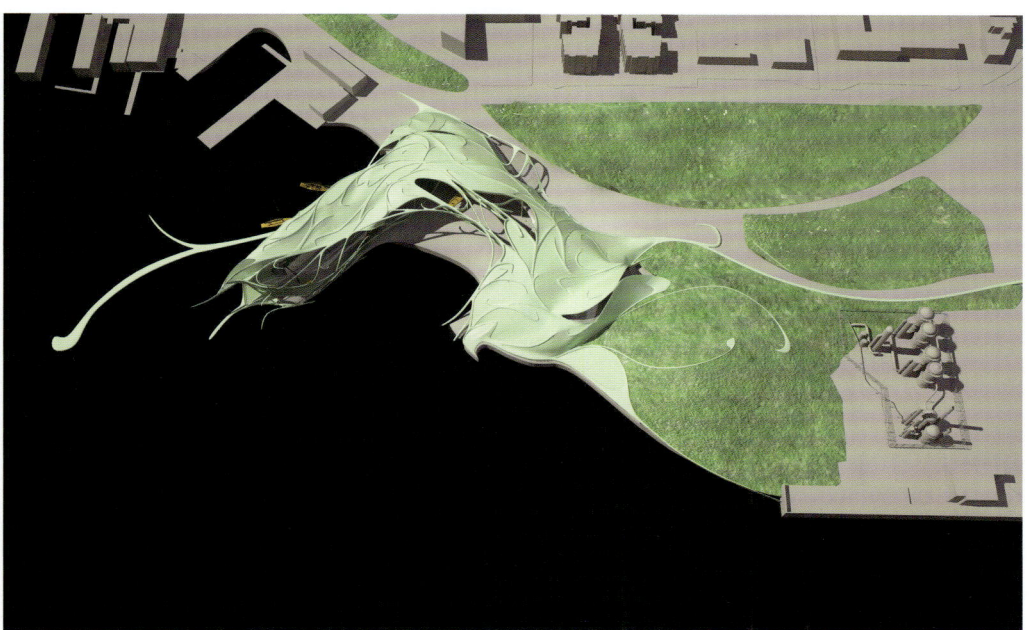

Aerial view of site showing ornamental connection between landscape, structure, and dock.

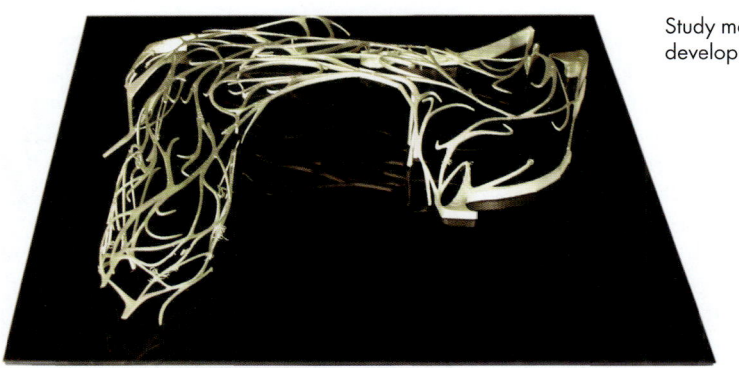

Study model used for development of ornament

View from water of hull fabrication hall and launch area

Soft Synthesis
Jonathon Cielo

Soft Synthesis, a design for a boat building factory, was accomplished primarily through the iterative process of digitally modeling a three-dimensional surface, flattening the surface into two-dimensional components, and prototyping and assembling the components into physical models. Developing a process that resulted in a physical object was critical because early on in the design two conceptual questions emerged as a focus for the project: how can architecture be informed by the surface design techniques of the high performance boating industry, and what is the role of the factory in contemporary architecture? It was only by emulating the assembly process that the latter question could be answered, and only by feeding this information back through the physical/digital loop could an answer to the former question emerge.

Like a racing boat hull, this building is designed as one continuous surface that transitions from an orthogonal factory-like form to a smooth, sensuous surface evocative of speed. Architecturally, this formal transition produces the effect of progression, movement, and performance. Programmatically, the evolution of form over the length of the building corresponds to the material evolution that occurs inside the building as raw materials are processed and fabricated into finished products. The form is unapologetically boat-like as if it were racing from land to water as a product of the technology that it houses.

In addition to being a factory itself, the building is conceived as an object that is built in an off-site factory. Carbon fiber bulkheads create a superstructure that mitigate the relationship between the irregular geometry of the exterior form and the regular geometry of the interior cranes and fabrication equipment. These bulkheads support a microstructure that frames over 13,000 differently sized and shaped panels. Because the panels are individually fabricated by computer numerical controlled (CNC) machines, their size and shape can indicate the resolution of curvature on the surface of the building. Small panels are therefore used at a high degree of curvature, while larger panels are used on flatter geometry. Functionally, this means that no panel bends more than one

degree. The aesthetic ambition of the project is strengthened by the solid/void palette of the glass and photovoltaic panels. The cladding of the surface reflects programmatic requirements while reinforcing the geometry, pixilated throughout to reiterate the scale of the part in relationship to the whole.

In the end, the project is a synthesis of a process that sought to resolve sculpting the form in conjunction with the design of the panels that articulated that form. As the incorporation of complex forms and surfaces becomes more and more pervasive in built architecture, the part-to-whole relationship and the process that establishes that relationship will become more and more meaningful. This project is a modest step towards uncovering that meaning.

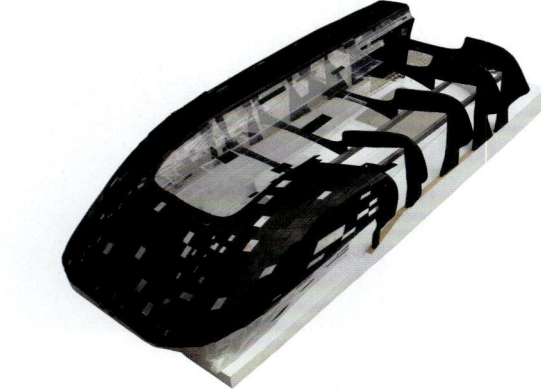

Detail model of sail loft wing of factory.

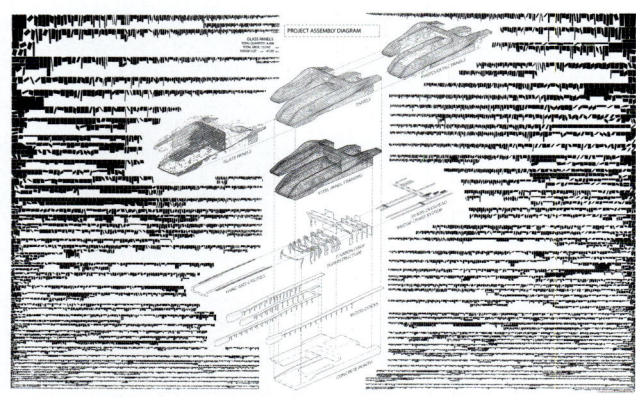

Isometric diagram and cut sheet for each facet of facade panelization.

Interior view of sail loft showing gantry overhead

View of factory at docks

View of factory from water

Factory at night showing varied opacity of panelized skin

Chris Bangle is an internationally renowned figure in the field of transportation design. He is best known for his work with BMW Group where he became the first American-born Chief of Design and was responsible for the design of BMW, MINI, and Rolls Royce automobiles. Bangle led cutting-edge concept car design with the Fiat "Junior." He continued pushing boundaries with the Z9 Gran Turismo and GINA at BMW. Bangle attended the Art Center College of Design in Pasadena, California where he earned a Bachelor of Science and master's degree in Industrial Design. He has since taught at the Graduate School of Design at Harvard and has been a juror at Yale School of Architecture. Upon leaving BMW in 2009 Bangle founded Bangle Designs where he investigates a broader spectrum of design.

Lise Anne Couture is a founder and partner of Asymptote Architecture. Their recently completed projects include The Yas Hotel in Abu Dhabi and 166 Perry Street in New York City. She received a Bachelor of Architecture from Carleton University in Canada and a Masters of Architecture from Yale University. She has taught at Columbia University, The Berlage Institute, the Graduate School of Design at Harvard, and Yale School of Architecture. With her firm, Ms. Couture has published work in *A+U*, *Assemblage*, *New Spirit in Architecture*, *Theory and Experimentation* as well as *Asymptote*, *Architecture at the Interval* a monograph. She was awarded a New York Foundation for the Arts fellowship and was Muschenheim Fellow at the University of Michigan.

Greg Foley is an award-winning author, illustrator, and creator. His work encompasses print, product design, performance, packaging, digital media, and graphic design. He is a creative director and designer of the media-bending *Visionaire* as well as *V Magazine*, and *VMAN*. Foley

153

attended the Rhode Island School of Design. In addition to serving as a guest critic at Yale School of Architecture, he teaches regularly at Parsons The New School for Design. He has published a number of children's books including the *Thank You Bear* series and *Willoughby & the Lion*.

Mark Foster Gage is assistant professor at Yale School of Architecture and an architect practicing in New York City where his firm, Gage/Clemenceau Architects, engages the continuing role of computation in generating new formal and aesthetic genres for architecture. They have exhibited work at the Museum of Modern Art in New York City and The Art Institute of Chicago. He holds a Bachelor of Architecture degree from Notre Dame and a Masters of Architecture from Yale University. At Yale he has taught and served as the coordinator of first year studio, and he taught advanced studios. In 2007 his firm was a finalist for the Museum of Modern Art/PS1 Young Architects Program. His projects, writings, and research have been published in *The New York Times*, the *Los Angeles Times*, *Vogue*, *Vogue Hommes International*, *Interior Design*, *Contra Progetti*, *A+U*, *Architecture*, *Metropolis*, *Architectural Record*, and *JAE*. He was on the editorial board of *Building Cities*, a Graham Foundation-funded book, and he co-edited *The Millennium House*, published by Yale School of Architecture and the Monacelli Press in 2004.

Frank Gehry founding partner of Frank O. Gehry & Associates based in Los Angeles, is one of the most prominent American architects and designers of the late twentieth and early twenty-first century. His buildings include the Guggenheim Museum in Bilbao, the Disney Concert Hall in Los Angeles, the California Aerospace Museum, the Fish Dance restaurant in Kobe, and the Entertainment Centre in Disneyland Paris among many more. Gehry is a graduate of the University Of Southern California School Of Architecture.

He has taught advanced studios at Columbia University and the Graduate School of Design at Harvard. At Yale School of Architecture he was the Davenport Visiting Professor for Spring 2010. Gehry has designed furniture for Knoll International, including the Bentwood Collection and the FOG stacking chair. In addition to buildings and furniture, he has designed jewelry, hats, sculpture, and sailboat interiors. He is an avid sailor.

Bill Kreysler is a founder of Kreysler & Associates (K&A), a custom molder of fiber reinforced products. K&A has won awards for excellence in the manufacture of Fiber Reinforced Polymer (FRP) architectural products, industrial products, and large-scale sculptures. Before founding K&A in 1982, Mr. Kreysler was Executive Vice President and Production Manager for the Performance Sailcraft Corporation (PSC), Northern California's largest manufacturer of sailboats at the time. Kreysler holds degrees in English and History from California State University, San Diego. He is the current chair of the Napa Valley Workforce Investment Board, Immediate Past President and Current Executive Committee Member of American Composites Manufacturers Association (ACMA), Past Director of the Society of the Plastics Industries Composites Institute, Chair of the Composite Fabricator Association Committee on Architectural Composites and Building Codes, and Chair of the Committee to Draft Guide Specifications and Recommended Practices for FRP Architectural Products. Kreysler races sailboats and serves on the St. Francis Yacht Club Board and Executive Race Committee.

Greg Lynn is the founder and principal of Greg Lynn FORM, an architecture office in Venice Beach, California, which designs buildings, products, and installations. Lynn is the Davenport Professor of Architecture at Yale University and holds degrees in architecture and philosophy from Miami University in Ohio and a Masters of

Architecture from Princeton University. He has taught and lectured around the world as the Professor of Spatial Conception and Exploration at the ETH (Swiss Federal Institute of Technology), Zurich, and as an adjunct assistant professor at Columbia University. In the fall of 2002 he became a professor at the Angewandte in Vienna, Austria. In addition, he is a studio professor at University of California, Los Angeles. *Time Magazine* named Lynn one of "100 Innovators for the Next Century" in 2001. He is the author of *Architectural Laboratories* published by Netherlands Architecture Institute in Rotterdam; *Folds, Bodies and Blobs: Collected Essays,* published by La Lettre Volée in Brussels; *Animate Form* and *Embryological House* both published by Princeton Architectural Press.

Adriana Monk is founder and Design Director of amDESIGN, specializing in transportation interiors for land, sea, and air. She is a graduate of Art Center College of Design, Pasadena, California. Ms. Monk has worked with automobile companies including Land Rover, Jaguar, Rolls Royce, and Ford Motor Company. Her interior work with Land Rover was the foundation for the 2002 Range Rover, and she developed the Phantom with Rolls Royce. Ford brought Ms. Monk on board to establish a luxury brand, during which time she developed four concept cars and the Lincoln MKS flagship. Most recently she has been Chief Designer of Wally Yachts, where she was responsible for interior concepts and detailing for both power boats and sailing yachts. She is a passionate sailor.

William Pearson is the Technical Director at North Sail's 3DL® manufacturing plant in Minden, Nevada. North was the first sailmaker to scientifically test stretch and fatigue in sailcloth; first to analyze sail shapes using computer flow codes; first to develop accurate computer air flow simulation for downwind sails at 100% scale;

first (and only) to build sails on a
full-size adjustable convex mold.
The North-patented process 3DL is
the world's dominant performance
sailmaking technology. In addition to
being technical director, as product
manager Pearson's sailmaking experience gives him an ideal background
for conveying the intricacies of high
performance sail manufacturing to his
salespeople. Pearson is a frequent
and competitive sailor.

155

O'Connor, Ruthann: p. 20 top

P, Alex: p. 85 center right

Pearson, William: p. 29 top right
(diagram courtesy of North Sails),
p. 29 bottom, p. 30, p. 31 top, center,
bottom, p. 32 top, center bottom,
p. 34

Rama: p. 22 (Image is licensed under
Creative Commons)

Ruji, Wynn: p. 85 top

Tan, Chiewhong: pp. 142–143 all
images

Truong, Quang: pp. 96–97 all images

Varner, Jessica: pp. 98–99 all images

Warchol, Paul: p. 135 center left
(photo by Paul Warchol Photography
Inc.)

Acknowledgements

The editors of the book and organizers of the studio at Yale would like to thank DuPont and Evans & Paul for donations of material, labor and knowledge; Alan Andrews, Janicki Industries, North Sails, and Sikorsky for informative tours of their cutting edge facilities; Dennis Conner for an unforgettable experience on-board Abracadabra; David Fenster, for filming and producing an excellent video on the studio; and visiting critics and jury members, including Robert Aish, Paola Antonelli, Chris Bangle, Mario Carpo, Bonnie Collura, Lise Anne Couture, Greg Foley, Kurt Forster, Frank Gehry, Meaghan Lloyd, Ari Marcopoulos, Florencia Pita, Marcelo Spina, and Stanley Tigerman whose input and expertise was critical to the process. A special thanks to those who contributed the writing and work that comprises this book, including the students of Greg Lynn's Studio and Mark Foster Gage's seminars and the professional contributors Chris Bangle, Lise Anne Couture, Greg Foley, Frank Gehry, Bill Kreysler, Adriana Monk, and William Pearson.

158